How to Design
Your Own Painting Projects

MICHELLE TEMARES

NORTH LIGHT BOOKS

CINCINNATI, OHIO
www.artistsnetwork.com

Library of Congress Cataloging-in-Publication Data

Temares, Michelle.

How to design your own painting projects / by Michelle Temares.

p. cm.

Includes index.

ISBN 1-58180-263-3 (pbk. : alk. paper)

1. Painting--Technique. I. Title.

ND1471 .T46 2003

751.4--dc21

Edited by Maureen Mahany Berger
Production coordinated by
Kristen Heller
Cover and interior design by
Joanna Detz
Page layout by Kathy Bergstrom
Photography by Christine Polomsky
and Tim Grondin

METRIC CONVERSION CHART

TO CONVERT	TO	MULTIPLY BY
Inches	Centimeters	2.54
Centimeters	Inches	0.4
Feet	Centimeters	30.5
Centimeters	Feet	0.03
Yards	Meters	0.9
Meters	Yards	1.1
Sq. Inches	Sq. Centimeters	6.45
Sq. Centimeters	Sq. Inches	0.16
Sq. Feet	Sq. Meters	0.09
Sq. Meters	Sq. Feet	10.8
Sq. Yards	Sq. Meters	0.8
Sq. Meters	Sq. Yards	1.2
Pounds	Kilograms	0.45
Kilograms	Pounds	2.2
Ounces	Grams	28.4
Grams	Ounces	0.04

ACKNOWLEDGMENTS

Many and heartfelt thanks to the following:

Kathy Kipp and Maureen Mahany Berger, North Light Books

Shirley Miller, Loew-Cornell

Susan Monahan, Masterson Art Products, Inc.

Chris Wallace, Walnut Hollow Farms

Faith Wismer, Winsor & Newton

Glenda Lallatin, Jean Chancelor and Lauren Powell, Plaid Enterprises

Anna Marie LaMont, Viking Woodcrafts

Lisa Brody Ritchey, Faber-Castell

Lavonne McCarty, Porcelain by Marilyn and Lavonne

Brad Podiak, Artograph

Sandra Cashman, Fiskars

Sara Naumann, Hot Off The Press

Anne Hevener, *Decorative Artist's Workbook*

Jay Sharp and Cathy Hickox, Creative Painting Convention

Mike Hartnett, Creative Leisure News

Paul Baumgarten, Esq.

The support and encouragement of the Decorative Artists of Long Island (DALI), a chapter of the Society of Decorative Painters

ABOUT THE AUTHOR

When I was a little girl I was continually torn between two careers. The first was to be the gift wrap lady at Macy's department store. What could be more glorious, I thought, than to wrap presents all day with as many bows and ribbons as you wanted. An early inkling, I suppose, of a career in design.

The second, and equally appealing choice, was to be an art teacher. The thought of spending all day teaching others how to create art was very exciting to me. Plus, I would have the key to the art room closet which was loaded with more construction paper and paste than I could use in an entire summer vacation.

As life would have it, I never did have to choose between a designing and a teaching career. I have been a product designer and an illustrator and spent two wonderful years as the principal of a product development, marketing and design firm. I am now privileged to be the Design Director of Plaid Enterprises, Inc., the world's leading manufacturer of craft and home décor products. And I have been blessed to teach many others how to draw and paint at national and regional art conventions, through local art societies, and by writing art instruction articles and books.

Through the years I have met many people who wanted to design their own decorative painting projects. They had been enjoying painting other artists'

designs but they longed to create their own original pieces. They didn't know how to start a design or how to see it through to a final product. The desire was great but so was the frustration, because design instruction was not available.

I began to develop a step-by-step design process, based on my own professional one, to help painters make their designing dreams come true. I tested it through classes at my own studio, Bella Michelle Studios, in Garden City, New York. I refined it further through classes at conventions. The results are now in your hands. Included are the tips, tricks and shortcuts I have learned through the years. I can say with assurance that if you study and follow the steps in this book, you will satisfy your deep urge to create beautiful decorative painting projects.

And, I still love to wrap presents!

With love and best wishes,

P.S. To contact me about this book or to share your thoughts about painting and design, please e-mail me at:

michelle@bellamichelle.com

You can visit me on the World Wide Web at: www.bellamichelle.com

Dedicated to
Mark Evan Temares
A Bright and
Shining Star

Table of Contents

Introduction...6

SECTION I: 7 EASY STEPS TO DESIGNING YOUR OWN PAINTING PROJECTS

CHAPTER 1
Designing & Painting Supplies...10

CHAPTER 2
What is Good Design?...16

CHAPTER 3
Step 1: Ideas & Inspiration...20

CHAPTER 4
Step 2: Using Reference Material...24

CHAPTER 5
Step 3: Choosing a Surface...32

CHAPTER 6
Step 4: Composition...37

CHAPTER 7
Step 5: Drawing...48

CHAPTER 8
Step 6: Developing a Color Scheme...55

CHAPTER 9
Step 7: Background Painting Techniques...65

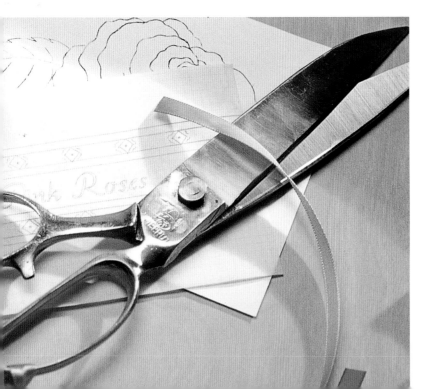

SECTION II: PUTTING YOUR DESIGN
SKILLS TO WORK ON PAINTED PROJECTS

PROJECT 1

The Greatest of These is Love ...82

PROJECT 2

Heavenly Garden ...94

PROJECT 3

Romance ...110

Resources ...124

Index ...126

Introduction

As soon as man satisfied his most basic needs, he began beautifying his surroundings with his own creativity. As manifested in the earliest cave paintings, the murals of Pompeii and the painted tinware of the early American settlers, the yearning to paint seems to be an inborn desire.

Before artists could buy paint at the art supply store, they created their own from the earth and from plants. Before they had high-quality manufactured paint brushes, they fashioned their own from sticks and animal hair. Before they had wood or tin surfaces to decorate, they used animal skins and cave walls.

As the center of our lives, our homes and families continue to provide prime opportunities for personal expression. What has become known as "decorative painting" has quickly become as popular as traditional canvas painting.

Traditional canvas painting is limited to a two-dimensional flat surface, usually rectangular, that we display on walls. Decorative painting, however, knows no limits! It can be on any surface from walls to floors to decorative accessories to furniture to fabric. It can be any size or shape. And unlike a traditional painting, it can be functional as well. As many a decorative painter has said, "If it doesn't move, watch out, 'cause I'm going to paint it!"

In recent years, many beautiful decorative painting books, complete with patterns and instructions, have been published. These are wonderful tools for learning and inspiration and should be a part of every decorative painter's library. Often, however, painters want to create their own original designs but they don't know how. Perhaps you want to increase your skills beyond re-creating the work of others, or you want a design that matches your living room or bedroom just perfectly, or you wish to create a custom gift for a very special person. This book is your answer.

How to Design Your Own Painting Projects takes you through an easy-to-follow seven-step design process. Right from the start you will be able to design your very own decorative painting projects. All aspects of design are covered in detail, with every step fully illustrated. This comprehensive book will teach you how to generate ideas, draw your design quickly and easily, develop gorgeous color schemes, create fabulous backgrounds and much more.

Michelle Temares, your author and guide, is the author of many decorative painting and art instruction articles, including the best-selling book, *Painting Floral Botanicals*, also from North Light Books. Michelle is the Design Director of Plaid Enterprises, Inc. She is an often-requested instructor at decorative painting and fine art conventions. She is also one of America's most popular designers specializing in the home decor, gift and hobby markets. Her work has been featured in department and specialty stores throughout the United States, South America and Europe.

In *How to Design Your Own Painting Projects* Michelle reveals her complete design process. Nothing is held back. Look for special bonus areas throughout the book labeled "Michelle's Design Secrets" for even more time- and money-saving shortcuts.

Decorative painting can change any surface from the ordinary to the extraordinary. The worthless can become priceless simply by adding a little of your time. No special talent or training is necessary. No expensive materials are needed. All that is required is some time to learn and a heart to create.

Think of the Possibilities

ANY SURFACE CAN BE BROUGHT TO LIFE WITH DECORATIVE PAINTING. CONSIDER THESE IDEAS FOR BEAUTIFUL AND MEMORABLE DECORATIVE PAINTING PROJECTS:

FURNITURE: NEW, UNFINISHED OR GARAGE SALE FINDS.

WALLS MURALS IN ANY ROOM OR HALLWAY OF YOUR HOME.

FLOORS: CREATE YOUR OWN PAINTED "RUG" FOR A FRACTION OF THE PRICE OF A STORE-BOUGHT RUG.

KITCHENS: TABLECLOTHS, PLACEMATS, NAPKINS, CHINA PATTERNS, KITCHEN TABLE AND CHAIRS, TILE, EVEN THE CABINETS. CREATE YOUR OWN PATTERN OR ADAPT ONE TO MATCH YOUR WALLPAPER OR DISHES.

BATHROOMS: TILE, SINK, CABINETRY, MIRROR, EVEN YOUR SHOWER CURTAIN OR DOOR.

BEDROOM: BEDS, SHEETS AND PILLOWCASES, COMFORTERS, CURTAINS, FURNITURE.

LIVING AREAS: FURNITURE, DECORATIVE ACCESSORIES, FIREPLACE MANTELS, INTERIOR DOORS.

PATIO/GARDEN: PLANTERS, SIGNS, OUTDOOR FURNITURE, EXTERIOR DOORS.

HOLIDAY IDEAS: DECORATIONS FOR WALLS AND TABLES, DOOR DECORATIONS, YARD DÉCOR, CHRISTMAS TREE ORNAMENTS AND SKIRTS.

GIFTS AND DECORATIVE ACCESSORIES: CANDLESTICKS, TRAYS, PLATES, BOWLS, BOXES, PHOTO ALBUMS AND SCRAPBOOKS.

FASHION: TRIM OR DESIGNS ON SHIRTS, BLOUSES, SKIRTS, NIGHTGOWNS, PAJAMAS AND CHILDREN'S CLOTHING, AND ACCESSORIES SUCH AS BUTTONS, SHOES, PURSES AND JEWELRY.

7 Easy Steps to Designing Your Own Painting Projects

What an exciting journey you are about to begin! Soon, you will be taking nothing more than a blank surface, brushes and some pigment, mixing them together with your dreams and imagination, and creating beautiful and inspiring decorative art. You can do it! The hardest part is beginning.

What stops most folks from beginning to paint or design is show-stopping, overwhelming, paralyzing fear. I'll let you in on a secret: It never goes away, not even for professional designers and artists. Each time I sit down to a blank page or canvas my heart races and my body tightens. Surely each previous success was a fluke that I cannot repeat. Soon, a blank piece of paper has more power than I do. "Listen," I say, "Who is in charge here? You or me?" Not sure of the answer, I give myself a pep talk. It never works, but I do it anyway.

So, what does work? How can you overcome fear and break through to your true creative self? You'll hear or read many strategies: Wear comfortable clothes, put on your favorite music, read an inspiring poem, light some candles for "atmosphere," etc. They won't work. They are just excuses to not begin working. My excuse for not beginning is to "prepare" my work area. When I resort to sharpening every pencil I own in the guise of "preparation," I know that fear is winning.

There is a way to overcome fear and to break through to your true creative self. It's simple, effective, and works every time. The solution is to just begin. Start with chapter one and follow the proven seven-step design process I will teach you. Fear is overcome by doing. There is no other remedy. Everything you'll need is already in you.

Design & Painting Supplies

Do you remember what you felt like when you had all new notebooks and school supplies in September? I remember being excited and full of anticipation. Art and design supplies make you feel like that, only better. They probably are of higher quality than the supplies you had as a child, and ultimately your supplies will produce exquisite artwork. Every fresh sharpening of my pencil, every new clean piece of paper, brings back that first-day-of-school excitement to me.

Unlike those for many hobbies and vocations, the supplies you will need for designing are simple, portable and inexpensive. In fact, you probably own many of them already. Several supplies I have listed are "must haves;" others are "nice to have." If you decide to purchase the "nice to haves" you will find that they will add a great deal of efficiency and convenience to your designing.

DESIGN SUPPLIES

Pencils, Sharpener, and Eraser: Must Haves

- 4H pencils (I suggest two pencils so that you are not constantly having to stop and sharpen your pencil.)

- Pencil sharpener (manual or electric, hand-held or wall-mounted)

- White vinyl eraser

Pencils vary by the hardness of their lead (actually, it's not lead but graphite). The softest pencils range from 2B to 6B. The higher the number, the softer the pencil. The harder pencils range from 2H to 6H. The higher the number, the harder the pencil. The HB pencil, as you might expect, is right in-between the two ranges. How hard or how soft varies by manufacturer. One manufacturer's 4H may be harder than another company's 2H; therefore, it's best to buy pencils from one manufacturer. This will ensure that you have a full range of hardnesses should you choose to buy several. Also, you do become accustomed to the pencil hardness or softness of a specific manufacturer and you will find that your hand pressure automatically adjusts to their pencils. Switching often between manufacturers can make your final design patterns inconsistent.

When sketching a scene, portrait or still life, HB or softer pencils are commonly used. They are easy to blend and provide a wide range of expression. For designing, however, a very hard pencil should be used. It provides precise lines that will not smudge. Accuracy is very much a part of the design process. Precise, smudge-free drawings help to develop and maintain accurate and consistent patterns.

The sharpener is a matter of personal preference. It's convenient to have one that contains the shavings; otherwise, the work area becomes quite messy.

I admit that I have strong prejudices about erasers. I have banished the popular gum eraser from my studio. It crumbles into endless, tiny pieces when used and makes a mess everywhere, and it's quickly depleted as well. Kneaded erasers are also quite popular. They don't make the mess of a gum eraser, but I find that they don't erase as well either. The perfect alternative is the white vinyl eraser. It erases thoroughly, leaving a clean, undamaged drawing surface, it doesn't make a mess, and it lasts a long time. For its usual price tag of under $1 (U.S.), you get a lot for your money.

Pencils and Sharpener: Nice to Have

A wonderful convenience to add to your design tools is a lead holder, leads, and the accompanying rotary sharpener. These replace standard drawing pencils. Lead holders are a long-time favorite of designers and architects. The primary advantage is that the lead can be sharpened to a much sharper point that stays sharp much longer, so there are fewer interruptions for sharpening. Lead holders are more comfortable to hold for long periods and are more economical over time because almost all of the lead is used, unlike standard pencils that are thrown away when they become too short to be comfortably held. A lead holder and package of twelve leads will each cost under $10 (U.S.). The lead holder lasts seemingly forever, and a package of twelve leads lasts me about a year with frequent use.

The lead used in a holder is too thin to work in a standard sharpener; besides, you don't want to sharpen and ruin the holder! A special rotary sharpener will also cost about $10 (U.S.). I have used mine constantly for about ten years and expect that it will last many more.

You may wish to purchase several lead holders and grades of lead. I dedicate one holder to 4H for designing and one each to HB and 2B for general sketching. Unfortunately, there is no way to tell which lead holder holds which lead. Therefore, for easy reference, I indicate the hardness/softness grade on a small piece of masking tape and place it around the bottom of the holder.

I have tried several brands over the years and prefer the Turquoise brand. The lead holder is well-balanced and feels comfortable in the hand. The lead is consistent for smooth drawing and the sharpener gives a nice sharp point.

Of all the "nice to haves" in this chapter, I encourage you most to purchase a lead holder, leads and accompanying sharpener. They have so many advantages over standard pencils.

Tracing Paper and Graph Vellum: Must Have

Preliminary drawings through final patterns are done on tracing paper. It's inexpensive and offers many designing advantages, demonstrated throughout this book. More expensive tracing paper is often heavier and therefore more opaque than cheaper paper. For designing, then, cheaper is better! Purchase the lightest weight and most transparent tracing paper you can find.

Graph vellum is tracing paper with a grid. It is similar to graph paper but it is translucent. It is used for making accurate templates of your surface as well as for accurate placement of motifs and lettering. Eight or ten squares to the inch are the most useful versions for designing.

The size paper or vellum to purchase depends on the size of your designs. If you plan to design small pieces, a smaller pad such as 8-inch x 10-inch (20cm x 25cm) will be fine. Larger pieces require a larger pad.

Tracing Paper and Graph Vellum: Nice to Have

Professional designers often purchase tracing paper and graph vellum by the roll instead of by the pad. Rolls contain several times more tracing paper than pads. If you plan on frequent designing, it will be more economical to purchase these items in rolls.

Moreover, if you would like to design and paint larger projects such as furniture or murals, rolls become a must. The largest pads typically available measure 16-inch x 20-inch. Rolls, however, are available in sizes as large as 48-inch X 50 yards.

Ruler: Must Have

Purchase a ruler marked with fractions of inches, (e.g. $\frac{1}{16}$, $\frac{1}{8}$, $\frac{1}{4}$, $\frac{1}{2}$) or smaller metric units (millimeters and centimeters). Again, the size to purchase depends on the design. Small designs can easily be handled with a 12-inch or 18-inch (30cm or 46cm) ruler; larger designs will need a longer ruler. For very large designs, a yardstick (meter) ensures the most accurate patterns.

Ruler: Nice to Have

The least expensive rulers are wood or plastic. The more expensive metal cork-backed rulers, however, offer many advantages. They are more carefully made and therefore more accurate. Their cork backing and heavier weight make them less likely to slip during use, and because the cork backing raises the ruler off the paper surface, ruled lines are sharper. Moreover, a metal ruler can be used as a straightedge for trimming final artwork.

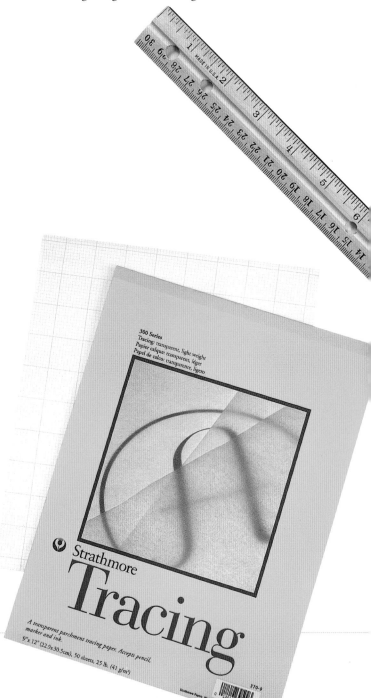

Colored Pencils

Colored pencils are used for preliminary layouts and color studies; therefore, the more colors you have, the better. Most brands offer at least one hundred different colors. I recommend Polychromos by Faber-Castell, which are available in one hundred twenty colors. Polychromos are the only oil-based colored pencil available. Only a small amount of oil is used in their manufacture, so there is no mess or smearing, but that small amount of oil makes these pencils much more blendable than any other colored pencil I have tried. Being able to quickly blend makes color studies progress much more quickly. These pencils are so wonderful to use that you will want to use them for permanent artwork as well.

Watercolor Paper

I am addicted to Winsor & Newton's watercolor paper. Due to its internal and external sizing, it does not need preparation or stretching and will not warp even with many layers of paint.

Watercolor paper is used for color inventories and color and technique studies. I like to use Winsor & Newton's paper for any permanent paintings I do as well.

The most versatile watercolor paper is 140-lb. (298gsm) cold-press; 140 lb. (298gsm) refers to the weight of a ream (five hundred sheets) of the paper. This is good midrange weight, heavy enough to withstand several layers of paint but light enough to be translucent when placed over a light box.

Cold-press refers to the texture. Watercolor paper is made in three textures: hot-press, cold-press and rough. Hot-press paper has a smooth finish, rough has a bumpy finish and cold-press is right in the middle with a slightly textured surface.

Prepared Acetate

Prepared acetate can be purchased at art supply stores but generally is not carried by craft stores. It is used for layout and final color and technique studies. Like regular acetate, prepared acetate is clear. However, due to special preparation by the manufacturer, the clear slick surface will accept paint. This allows for quick and easy testing of layout, color and technique without having to waste time transferring the pattern.

Painting Supplies

Masterson Sta-Wet Palette

I cannot paint beautifully in acrylics without a Masterson Sta-Wet palette. Acrylic paints dry very rapidly. If the paint begins to dry, which happens almost immediately without a Masterson Sta-Wet palette, it is difficult to load the brush, even more difficult to move the loaded brush across the painting surface and almost impossible to blend colors. Trying to work with partially dry paints produces choppy and unattractive results. A Masterson Sta-Wet palette will keep acrylic paints moist for up to several weeks. This not only makes painting easier but more economical, because paint is never wasted or thrown out at the end of a painting session.

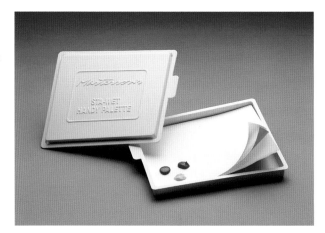

Brushes

I highly recommend Loew-Cornell brushes, especially the Arttec sable brushes for projects on paper and the La Corneille synthetic brushes for all other surfaces. These brushes really stand up to vigorous and constant use. I also prefer Loew-Cornell's brushes because they maintain a sharp edge, hold a good deal of paint and need less reloading. They are also moderately priced.

Paint

The projects in this book were painted with FolkArt by Plaid. FolkArt paints tend to be a bit thicker than other brands of bottled acrylic paint. This thick, creamy consistency provides excellent coverage, so usually only one basecoat is necessary. Highlights and shades build faster as well. FolkArt paints are intermixable--providing you with an endless variety of color.

Miscellaneous Supplies

- **Slide holder sheets and loose-leaf notebook** To hold slides and paint inventory chips. Slide sheets can be purchased at photography stores.

- **Water basins** At least two: one for clean water and one for cleaning dirty brushes.

- **Light box or wax-free transfer paper** For transferring patterns to the painting surface.

- **Paper towels** To blot excess water from brushes.

- **Palette knife** For easier paint mixing.

CHAPTER TWO

What is Good Design?

What is good design? Perhaps no other question has been so hotly debated in the art world. Some say good design is innovative or cutting-edge. Some say it has to be classical. Some just say they know it when they see it. As designers, however, we need something more concrete: something we can keep in our minds as we design. Regardless of style or purpose, good design accomplishes several goals.

GOOD DESIGN

EVOKES EMOTION OR A MOOD

We gaze and think, "How beautiful" or "How moving" or even, "Gee, wish I had thought of that." We respond not only with our minds but also with our hearts.

What emotion do you desire your design to evoke? Serenity? Joy? Tranquility? Excitement? Your choice of design elements such as color, composition, line and balance all work together to create a mood. To do this successfully, they need to work in harmony and not fight each other.

This greeting card for a father successfully combines a feeling of masculinity with the underwater mood of a favorite male hobby: fishing.

IS FOCUSED

Good design never confuses the viewer. It tells your eye exactly where to look, establishing a center of interest and then leading the eye naturally from element to element. There is no strain or confusion, but rather, flow, continuity and consistency of presentation.

The red rose immediately draws the eye to a clear center of interest in this greeting card. Consistent color and technique create continuity throughout the design.

HAS UNITY

The individual elements of a good design work together to support the whole. Background colors complement subject colors. Motifs make sense when grouped together. The top and sides of the piece form a balanced composition. All design elements complement one another in such a way that they seem to have always existed together.

   This Christmas stationery grouping, through echoed color and motif, is beautifully complementary. Each piece works well on its own as well as in unity with other members of the group.

IS CONFIDENT

A good design speaks boldly—but boldly is not the same as loudly. Good design tells a story clearly and without hesitation. The underlying drawing is accurate, the color schemes are in harmony and the composition is in balance. The designer knows her tools well and uses them to their best advantage. She uses them with confidence.

   This portrait, of my handsome nephew Ryan, shows confidence with both material and technique. It utilizes the full range of the pastel medium, while the painting's darks and lights are placed accurately and with assurance. This painting shows neither fear nor hesitation.

GETS REMEMBERED

The design may not be to your personal taste. It's modern; you prefer traditional. Or it's very colorful but you prefer softer hues. Regardless, your memory of that particular design lingers in your mind. Good design does that: it sticks with you.

   This tabletop set's nostalgic mood and color scheme make it a memorable part of any kitchen décor.

HOW TO ACHIEVE GOOD DESIGN

As a song can be broken down to individual notes, good design can also be broken down into individual notes or elements. When arranged correctly, notes can become beautiful music. The same individual notes may be used from piece to piece, but the combinations, and therefore the end results, are infinite.

The following elements are indispensable to good design.

LINE

Line sets the tone of a piece. Designs with a predominantly straight horizontal or vertical emphasis and little curvature are formal and strong. When a piece has predominantly curvy lines it appears more relaxed and casual.

This greeting card, depicting a choir of multicultural angels, exhibits bold line by arranging the angels into the shape of a Christmas tree.

PROPORTION

When individual elements are in proportion to the whole, the design looks harmonious. When elements are too small, they appear lost. When they are too large, they appear to burst out of the space.

For each print in this textile grouping, the size of the space it would occupy was considered. Larger pieces like the comforter can support a larger pattern. Smaller pieces like the dust ruffle require a pattern with smaller scale.

BALANCE

Think of an old-fashioned scale. When the weight on each side is equal, the scale is in balance. Design works much the same way. Balance must be achieved in all areas of the design including line, proportion, rhythm, texture and color.

This bold vest print looks suitable on the model due to the balance achieved in both color and layout.

RHYTHM

For a piece to have rhythm there must be variety in the size and shape of the elements. For example a design of all one flower, in one size and orientation, would have a very dull rhythm. But when the elements vary in size and shape the design achieves interest created in part by the rhythm.

The variety and color of the fruit in this piece, as well as their mixed groupings, achieve rhythm in what could have been a dull print.

TEXTURE

Texture is the surface appearance of the piece. Does the design appear to be smooth like the surface of a rose petal, or rough and bumpy like perhaps an alligator's skin? Texture can add tremendous interest to a piece, but it works best when it is used judiciously. Too many textures in one piece can result in visual confusion.

The addition of texture to this bathing suit print introduces an entirely new dimension to the look.

HARMONY

A design is harmonious when no single element unintentionally stands out or interferes with the overall painting. The design is in proportion to the surface space. The colors do not fight one another for attention. The rhythmic pattern flows effortlessly. The texture is not overwhelming. Everything works together as beautifully as a symphony.

This kitchen textile print successfully combines several different looks in one design. Due to proper scale, proportion, balance, color and complementary motifs, the result is an interesting and appealing design.

COLOR

Studies have shown repeatedly that color is the first design element viewers notice. Colors can make or break a design. When they fight, the screaming is almost audible. When they cooperate, there is peace. A color scheme must include shades that interact well with each other while supporting the design as a whole.

This wallpaper pattern uses a classic yellow and violet complementary color scheme using golds and plums. The blue accents add a touch of visual relief without detracting from the whole.

CHAPTER THREE

Step 1: Ideas and Inspiration

YOUR DECORATIVE PAINTING C.E.O.

Drawing ability, design expertise and painting techniques are important skills for designing. But the designer's real stock in trade is not interesting compositions, unusual background techniques or striking color schemes. Her most important possession and greatest asset is her creativity.

The first step in designing your own decorative painting projects is to decide on a design concept. Inspired ideas lead to exciting and successful design. Trite, overused concepts lead to design that gets lost in a sea of sameness.

Perhaps the greatest intimidator for the beginning designer is a blank piece of paper. Precious hours may be wasted staring down at the blank surface and wracking your brain for "the big idea." The secret to avoiding this frustrating and discouraging picture is to make inspiration and creativity an ongoing and integral part of your life. You'll then find that you get more ideas than you'll ever have time to use.

I do this with something I call The Decorative Painter's C.E.O.™, that is, The Decorative Painter's Creative Expression Organizer™. This chapter gives you a tour of The Decorative Painter's C.E.O. You can purchase a Decorative Painter's C.E.O. through me. Or, you can follow the instructions in this chapter and make your own.

The Decorative Painter's C.E.O. is a combination sketchbook, inspiration recorder, project planner, idea generator, color scheme tester and study guide all in one. In short, it's a portable, working studio that can and should go everywhere you go. It becomes a part of your daily wardrobe just like a purse or briefcase.

Using your Decorative Painter's C.E.O. regularly will increase your creativity, enthusiasm, and design skills. You'll never have to stare endlessly again at a blank piece of paper because your Decorative Painter's C.E.O. will be overflowing with ideas that you can't wait to try.

Inside my Decorative Painter's C.E.O. are six sections: Inspiration, Ideas, Design Plans, Sketches, Palettes, and Studies.

IDEAS & INSPIRATION

Ideas

It's important to have a pen and paper with you at all times, even when you're sleeping! New ideas seem to come at the least expected moments. If they aren't written down right away, they are often lost. I used to keep a pen and paper in my purse, in the car, by the side of my bed and so forth, but I find that I can lose these individual snippets or can't find them when I need them. Including a New Ideas Section in my Decorative Painter's C.E.O. keeps my ideas organized and accessible.

Tip

KEEP A LOADED CAMERA WITH YOU AT ALL TIMES. DISPOSABLE ONES ARE PERFECT. THEY ARE INEXPENSIVE AND FIT EASILY INTO A PURSE.

Inspiration

Pasted into this section are photographs of flowers, country scenes and other images that that strike me as beautiful and encourage me to create. This section also includes pictures from magazines and catalogs, fabric swatches, snippets of interesting specialty papers and anything else that makes me suck in my breath and say, "Wow, that's gorgeous!" When I am feeling unmotivated to design, glancing through this section always gets my adrenaline pumping and my legs heading straight for my painting table.

Images for your Inspiration section are all around you. Places to look include parks, beaches, gardens, art and natural history museums, books and magazines, catalogs, fashion layouts, fabric swatches, wallpaper books, retail stores and more. Look for images that inspire you, but also look for details that can be adapted for future designs such as themes, motifs, patterns, textures and color schemes.

DESIGN PLANS, SKETCHES & PALETTES

Design Plans

Here's where I work out the details of a project. The idea may have come from a note jotted in the Ideas section or a detail from one of the images in the Inspiration section.

A page from this section can include:

- A sketch of the surface I want to use and the name and contact information for the supplier.

- Notes on the theme for the piece, e.g., garden scene with trellis and white wrought iron bench; fall still life with pumpkins, tossed leaves and dried grasses.

- Enlarged sketches of the surface indicating possible design layout options.

- Motif sketches.

- Notes and/or swatches for color schemes.

- Notes and/or swatches for background techniques.

- Anything else that I may want to remember, including lettering ideas, varnish and finishing plans, etc.

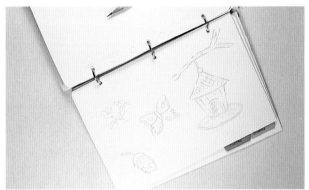

Sketches

This is the place to capture visual images, especially when using a camera is not convenient. It's also a place to practice drawing skills. In some places, such as museums, a sketchbook is essential because photography is not allowed. My favorite places to sketch are parks, gardens, country fairs and natural history museums. Date your sketches and you will have a wonderful visual journal of places and special moments from your life.

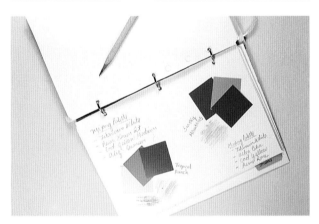

Palettes

This is where I keep color swatches and color scheme plans. I include photos from nature, yarn and floss swatches, and paint swatches based on artwork, nature or fashion. Anything that has striking or beautiful color combinations that can be used in future projects goes into this section. It's also a place to keep a record of paint mixing recipes for colors you want to mix again and successful color schemes from past projects.

STUDIES

Studies are test paintings for final projects. They provide the opportunity to try out color schemes, lighting plans and painting techniques without making a mess of your final piece. Very often this section uses material from the previous sections in your Decorative Painter's C.E.O. For example: photos from the Inspiration section may have been incorporated into a design concept in the Ideas section, which is worked out in more detail in the Design Plans and Sketches sections using color schemes from the Palette section. Everything is then combined for a test painting in the Studies section.

How to Make Your Own Decorative Painter's C.E.O.

Materials:

- 6 tabbed dividers. Label them as follows:
  Inspiration
  Ideas
  Design Plans
  Sketches
  Palettes
  Studies

- Paper to fit each section. Your choice of lined or unlined.

- 3 one- or two-inch (3 to 5cm) loose-leaf rings

- Decorative front and back covers. Mat board works well. Cut with a sharp craft knife.

- HB or #2 pencil and ¼ yard (23cm) of thin ribbon.

- Fiskars® Craft Hand Drill.

Instructions

1. Decorate your cover to reflect your own style and inspiration.

The cover of my Decorative Painter's C.E.O. is Winsor & Newton 140-lb. (298gsm) cold-press watercolor paper that I painted with blended washes of pale pink, yellow and blue. The border was cut with Fiskars Regular Paper Edgers in the deckle edge pat-

tern. The paper was then glued to a slightly larger piece of Fiskars pastel pink card stock to create a pink border, and then glued to white mat board. Since pink roses are one of my favorite flowers and I love vintage-look florals, I pasted pink roses cut from a vintage greeting card on a square of pin-dot vellum from Hot Off The Press, Inc. A pretty white border was created with white ribbon from Offray.

Your cover can be hand-painted, stamped, appliqued or stencilled. Or simply use a pretty fabric or specialty paper. Choose what inspires you.

2. Enclose your labeled tabs and paper within the covers in the order indicated at left, or the order that works best for you. Using the Fiskars Craft Hand Drill, drill three equally-spaced holes at the top of the book and insert loose-leaf rings. The rings will provide flexibility, allowing you to add or remove pages as needed.

3. Glue ribbon to the eraser end of a pencil and tie the other end to the far-right loose-leaf ring if you are right-handed or the far-left if you are left-handed. (I even painted the barrel of my pencil with FolkArt Acrylic paint in Sweetheart Pink to match my cover.)

Now that you have a portable studio, no good idea or design opportunity should pass you by!

CHAPTER FOUR

Step 2: Using Reference Material

During my first month in art school I was surprised by a statement repeated by several of my professors: "A designer" they said, "is only as good as his or her reference material." "How could that be?" I thought. "Isn't creativity more important? What about drawing skills? Aren't they more important?" As the semester continued, I discovered that my professors were absolutely right.

The vast majority of us are not able to draw "out of our heads." The level of detail needed is not stored in our memories. For example, I know that a poinsettia is red with pointy leaves. However, I need to look at a photo or live poinsettia to determine the exact shape of the leaves, the direction and placement of the veining, and the leaf arrangement in relation to other leaves and the stem. Without this information I am unable to make an accurate drawing.

Reference material can be actual objects, photographic images or live models. Seventeenth-century Dutch artists painted floral still lifes over the course of many months as they waited for each specimen to bloom. Monet painted the flowers and architectural structures from his gardens at Giverny, France. Norman Rockwell used his friends and neighbors as models, and he maintained an extensive collection of costumes and props.

Where to Find Reference Material

All over! Some of the most popular sources are:

- Your own photographs
- Art books
- Magazines
- Newspaper ads
- Household objects
- Antiques
- Catalogs
- Post cards

But the best source by far is your Decorative Painter's C.E.O., especially the Inspiration and Sketches sections.

How Reference Photography Differs from Personal Photography

Taking pictures for design reference is much different from taking pictures to capture memories or beautiful scenery. In fact, your reference photos may be far from beautiful. Personal photography is about capturing a moment. Design reference photography is about capturing detail. With personal photography, the photograph is the end product. With design photography, the painted design is the end product. The photograph is a tool to help you get there.

Tips for Taking Reference Photos

- For reference photos to be useful they must be in focus, be well-lit and show detail.

- Many shots of the same subject may be needed: near, far, front, back, side, etc. It's not unusual to use an entire roll of film on one subject.

- A good set of reference photos can be used again and again. Film is inexpensive; take the extra shots.

- Try to take reference photos in the early morning or late afternoon, when the light is most interesting. Good light produces saturated colors and prominent shadows. These extra pieces of information will make color selection and value planning much easier.

- Manual focus is better than automatic focus. The lens of an automatic camera may focus on something other than what you wanted to capture. The resulting photo will be useless if the subject you wanted to capture is blurry beyond recognition.

- Use the correct film speed for the lighting conditions. 200 ASA is a good standard for most outdoor conditions. If the light is very low, or the day very overcast, switch to a faster film such as 400 ASA that will capture more light.

Good and Better

BETTER

This clear, close-up also shows three different views of the flower head, as well as the stem and growth habit.

GOOD

This photo is clear and close-up. However, it shows only one view of the flower head.

GOOD

A clear, closeup with beautiful color shows flower heads and leaves.

BETTER

This shot provides much more information. It includes three views of flower heads, three buds, stems, leaves and sepals.

Capture Many Types of Reference

Composition

With well-planned pictures such as this one, the design practically paints itself. The composition was planned through the lens of my camera.

Scenic

Scenes with a definite foreground, middle ground and background make excellent scenic and mural references.

People and Animals

Portraits, candids and action shots are all worth capturing. People in costume or native dress can add special interest to a design.

Floral

The most popular motif in home decorating is the floral. Record a range of flowers throughout the growing season.

Seasonal

Seasonal designs are planned far in advance of the season. Unless you have appropriate references in your files, it will be difficult to design for Christmas during July, or for Thanksgiving during April.

Motif and Detail

I loved the idea of flower pots decorating the exterior wall of a house. This picture will remind me of that concept as well as the beautiful detail in the balcony railing. Photograph even small details. Many of my borders are inspired by small motifs I find when I'm looking carefully.

Color

Nature is a favorite color reference guide for many designers.

Texture

Pictures of brick, stone, tile and gravel will help tremendously when rendering these surfaces. In this picture, both the layout of the stone and the wide range of values are recorded for future use.

HOW TO ORGANIZE YOUR REFERENCE MATERIAL

Soon you will have pictures, clippings and other reference materials overflowing your shelves and countertops. It's time to set up a filing system.

Organize your material by subject, then place each subject in its own folder. Folders are most accessible when stored in a filing cabinet. When a file becomes overstuffed, it's time to break it down into subcategories. For example, an "Animals" file can be broken down into wild animals, domestic animals, animals that fly and animals that live in water. Sometimes these categories may need to broken down even further if it's one of your frequently collected subjects.

As my file subjects grew, I found it advantageous to maintain a master list. This helped me to organize my material and avoid duplication, especially of overlapping categories. I also note any relevant cross references next to each subject. This helps me to locate a subject that could fit into more than one category. For example, next to "Evergreens," the note says "See Trees." Otherwise, I might search under "Christmas," which is also a logical fit.

Reference Categories

Here are my frequently used reference categories. Use these to begin setting up your own files.

- Animals

- Children's motifs

- Color

- Design periods
  (Victorian, Art Deco, Art Nouveau, etc.)

- Food (general, fruit, vegetables, etc.)

- Floral (one folder per flower)

- Gardening

- Holiday/Seasonal
  (Christmas, Fall, Spring, Winter, Summer)

- Kitchen and bath

- Layout

- Music

- People
  (children, adults, old-fashioned, in costume, etc.)

- Scenic

- Sports

- Transportation

- Toys and games

- Water and sky

- Western

Copyright

In addition to your own photographs, your reference files may include other visual examples, such as greeting cards, fabric and wallpaper swatches, magazine and catalog clippings and so on. While any of these may be used for inspiration, only your own photographs may be copied for design purposes.

Copyright is simply what its name says: the right to copy. Only the copyright holder has the right to use or copy an image. An image is copyrighted as soon as it is created. The copyright © symbol is not required to establish ownership, although it does remind others of your legal claim. All images, whether published or unpublished, professional or amateur, are the property of the individual or company that either created them or purchased the copyright. They may not be copied for any reason without permission.

Some people think that an image or text is protected only if it's owned by a large company such as Disney or Hallmark. This is not true. Copyright protection is the same for individuals as it is for corporations. Another myth is that it's OK to copy if one changes the wording of a text or the colors in a design. You may have heard that as long as the altered version differs from the original by at least ten percent—or twenty-five percent, or some other magic number—then it does not violate any copyright restrictions, but this is completely untrue.

In brief, if you are not the copyright holder, you may not copy text or an image whether in whole or in part. Penalties for copyright violation are very stiff, starting at $15,000 (U.S.). Designers and companies are vigilant about protecting their copyrights and will sue if violations occur. After all, their livelihoods depend on the sale of their designs.

This is good news for you as a designer. Once you create a design, you own it exclusively. No one else may copy it unless you give written permission. If you live in the United States, you may want to register your copyright with the United States Copyright Office. This enables you to prove the date of creation. Registering a copyright is simple and inexpensive. In most cases, all that is required is the completion of a one-page form and a $30 (U.S.) registration fee. More information may be found at www.loc.gov/copyright/.

CHAPTER FIVE

Step 3: Choosing a Surface

Surfaces are exciting! The endless variety in material, shape, size, proportion and style makes it almost impossible to choose. There are surfaces available for every taste and budget. If you are like most decorative painters, you already have—or will soon have—quite a stash waiting for your artistic hand. Still, most of us find it hard to resist buying one or two more that we "just have to have."

CHOOSING A SURFACE

When choosing a surface, consider the style of the design as well as its intended function. Delicate Victorian designs often look pleasing on a Victorian style porcelain surface. Masculine designs lend themselves to more sturdy surfaces such as wood or metal. Contemporary designs look best on surfaces with modern lines while traditional designs work best on classically-styled pieces.

Consider, also, how the piece will be used. Glass lends itself well to serving pieces. Wooden chests and boxes provide excellent storage. Metal, due to its durability when finished with an outdoor varnish, makes excellent garden décor projects. Papier-mâché, due to its low cost, is an excellent option for small gifts and paint-to-sell items.

WOOD

ADVANTAGES

Wide selection of functional & decorative pieces

Durable

DISADVANTAGES

Requires some preparation

Larger pieces can be heavy

METAL

ADVANTAGES

Requires little preparation

Lightweight

Durable

DISADVANTAGES

More limited selection

PORCELAIN

ADVANTAGES

Beautiful luster

May have embossed details

Pieces may be fired on the inside for functionality

Requires little preparation

DISADVANTAGES

Fragile

More expensive than most surfaces

GLASS

ADVANTAGES

Wide selection

Inexpensive

Requires little preparation

Clear glass requires no pattern transfer

DISADVANTAGES

Fragile

CANVAS

ADVANTAGES

Durable

Inexpensive

Requires no preparation

DISADVANTAGES

Limited selection

CHOOSING A SURFACE, *continued*

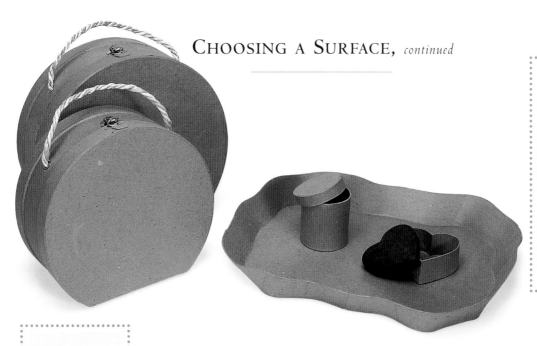

WHERE TO PURCHASE SURFACES

Over the past twenty or so years, an entire industry has developed to serve the surface needs of decorative painters. Surfaces from these companies have ample design area and are ready to paint with little or no preparation.

Surfaces may be purchased at local art and craft supply stores. Mail order and Internet shopping offer an even greater variety. Also—do not miss national and regional decorative painting conventions. Along with classes, displays and special events, conventions offer a large shopping area known as the trade floor, where you'll find a wide variety of companies and surfaces all in one place. Be sure to wear comfortable shoes and bring your credit card!

Here are recommendations for sources:

Art and Craft Stores

Walnut Hollow Farm, Inc.
1409 State Road 23
Dodgeville, WI 53533
(800) 950-5101
www.walnuthollow.com
wood products

Arty's Silk Collection

The Janlynn Corporation
34 Front St.
P.O. Box 51848
Indian Orchard, MA 01151
(800) 445-5565
www.janlynn.com
silk garments, accessories and home décor items

Mail Order/Internet

Viking Woodcrafts, Inc.
1317 8th St. SE
Waseca, MN 56093
(800) 328-0116
www.vikingwoodcrafts.com
large variety of surfaces

Porcelain by Marilyn & Lavonne
3687 W US 40
Greenfield, IN 46140
(317) 462-5063
white satin porcelain surfaces

Decorative Painting Conventions

Society of Decorative Painters
393 N. McLean Blvd.
Wichita, KS 67203
(316) 269-9300
www.decorativepainters.org

Heart of Ohio Tole, Inc. (HOOT)
P.O. Box 626
Reynoldsburg, OH 43068
(614) 863-1785
www.heartofohiotole.org

New England Traditions
N. Main St.
Marlborough, CT 06447
(800) 878-0029
www.newenglandtraditions.com

Creative Painting
P.O. Box 80720
Las Vegas, NV 89180
(702) 221-8234
http://hometown.aol.com/vegaspaint/index.html

UNEXPECTED SOURCES

Mass Market Discounters

Take regular walks through Wal-Mart, K-Mart and Target and you'll find some terrific and inexpensive surfaces. The home office department often has wood pieces that make great gifts for both women and men. The housewares department has all sorts of glassware. Candy jars and covered casserole dishes make especially nice design surfaces. The kitchen department offers metal baking tins and pans. Picture frames with wide borders make great surfaces, as do fabric- or paper-covered photograph albums. Keep your design eye open and check every department.

Garage Sales and Flea Markets

Garage sales and flea markets are ideal hunting grounds for economical and interesting surfaces. Often these pieces are one-of-a-kind.

Don't let a less-than-brand-new appearance scare you away. Painted wooden pieces can be sanded smooth or stripped. Rusty metal can have character. Glassware can be brightened up with cheery motifs or colors. Old linens make beautiful painting surfaces; small stains often can be hidden by a newly painted design. Inspect items carefully before purchasing to make sure you can fix or live with any flaws. Garage sale and flea market purchases usually are not returnable.

Office Supply Stores

Designers can find hidden treasures in office supply stores. These include bulletin boards (yes, you can paint on cork!), dry-erase boards (you can paint on these too), binders and photo albums, metal file organizers, metal wastebaskets and home office accessories.

Garden Centers

A clay pot is a classic decorative painting surface, but also try painting flowers or garden scenes on trowels, wide metal shovels, metal watering cans or wheelbarrows.

Hardware Stores

Some great painting surface buys here include slate and ceramic tiles, metal sheeting, smooth plywood, unfinished cabinet doors and knobs. Hardware stores are also great places to find painting surfaces for gifts for the men in your life such as metal saws and blades (you may want to dull these with use first) and metal tool chests.

CHAPTER SIX

Step 4: Composition

Composition refers to the arrangement of all parts of a design. The design elements discussed in chapter two all contribute to the composition, and must work together harmoniously to achieve a successful design.

Unlike traditional painting, which is usually confined to a flat, rectangular surface, decorative painting may be done on a variety of three-dimensional surfaces that present unique compositional challenges. Designers must consider the composition of each surface plane as well as the composition of the whole piece. Line, shape, color, value (the lightness or darkness of a color), texture, and the use of positive and negative space affect the sense of balance necessary to a good composition.

WHAT MAKES A GOOD COMPOSITION?

DON'T
The sides of the surface aren't balanced vertically and horizontally, nor is the surface as a whole.

DO
Each side of the surface is balanced vertically and horizontally, as is the surface as a whole.

WHAT MAKES A GOOD COMPOSITION? *continued*

DON'T

Achieving balance by dividing the surface into two equal parts is not very effective. Dividing a design in the middle either horizontally or vertically results in a painting that looks as if it were cut in half.

DO

Be sure to make the sides of your design asymmetrical so that it's more interesting.

DON'T

A series of non-overlapping shapes is boring.

DO

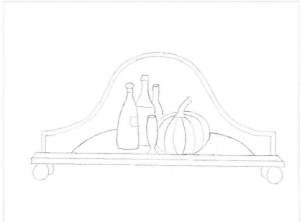

Create depth and perspective by overlapping shapes.

THE CENTER OF INTEREST

Establish a single center of interest. This is the most important area of the design and the place you would like the viewer to look at first. The center of interest can be a figure, a group of figures, an object, a flower or a bunch of flowers, a single motif or even an area of more intense color. The center of interest has more detail than the rest of the design. The most visually interesting designs are those in which the center of interest is not in the center of the piece, but slightly off-center.

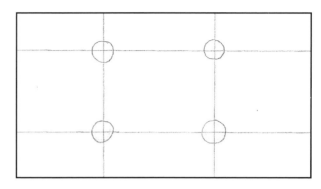

The Golden Mean

The Golden Mean

Through the centuries artists have often determined the center of interest in a painting by using the Golden Mean, a mathematical formula used by the ancient Greeks and Romans to determine the most pleasing aesthetic proportions. To find the Golden Mean, visually divide the surface into thirds vertically, and again horizontally to make nine equal parts. The four center points at which the lines intersect are considered the best locations for a center of interest. Placing your center of interest at any of these four intersections will help ensure a successful composition.

DON'T

Positive space refers to the area occupied by the figures and objects in a design; *negative space* refers to the area around those figures. Objects that are too evenly spaced form boring compositions.

DO

Those designs with more varied negative spaces are far more interesting.

DON'T

It is ineffective to use lines that lead the viewer out of the picture.

DO

Use lines to lead the viewer into the picture.

DON'T

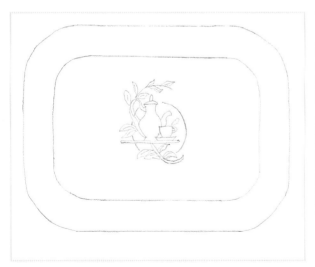

Make sure your design is neither too small nor too big for your surface.

DO

Create a design that is in proportion to the space.

DON'T

Avoid "line ups" and "alleys" that create unintended holes or striped patterns.

DO

Put your design together so that its elements flow in an interesting, yet random pattern.

DON'T

Avoid lettering that doesn't match the design.

DO

Any lettering should match the design in both proportion and style.

COMPOSITIONAL CHOICES

When in doubt, choose one of these classic forms to ensure a successful composition.

TRIANGULAR

C SHAPE

S SHAPE

L SHAPE

PUTTING IT TOGETHER

Often the main design will be on the largest plane of the surface. Usually this is the top or front of the surface. Design this area first. Then, pull motifs from this section to continue a design for the remaining areas.

Suggestions for Compositional Arrangements

Use color to form complementary stripes or geometric patterns.

Repeat motifs pulled from the main design.

Enlarge or reduce selected motifs.

Develop borders using motifs from the main design.

44

STEPS TO DESIGNING YOUR COMPOSITION

Make A Template

The size, shape and proportions of the surface have a significant impact on the composition. Therefore, the first step to designing the composition is to make a template or outline tracing of each side of the surface.

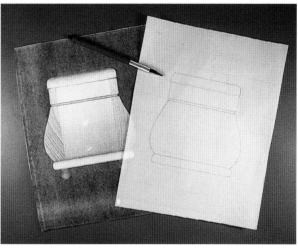

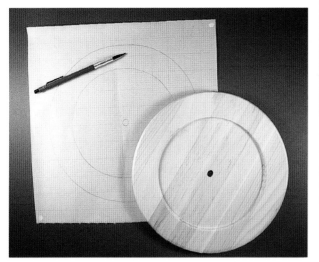

An easy way to make a template is to simply trace the outline of the item onto tracing paper. An accurate template can also be made using a ruler and graph vellum. Carefully measure the dimensions of each side of the surface and draw the shapes on the graph vellum. Use a ruler for any straight lines. The measured boxes on the graph vellum are a great help in ensuring accuracy.

When making a template of irregular surfaces, make a photocopy of the item and then trace the photocopy onto the graph vellum. This method is also helpful when making templates of items with inner rims or borders that are difficult to trace.

Michelle's Design Secrets

IF AN ITEM IS TOO LARGE TO FIT ON THE PHOTOCOPIER, PHOTOCOPY IT IN SECTIONS AND THEN TAPE THE SECTIONS TOGETHER FOR A COMPLETE COPY.

IF YOU WOULD LIKE EACH SIDE OF A SURFACE TO HAVE THE SAME DESIGN, YOU WILL NEED ONLY ONE TEMPLATE. FOR EXAMPLE, A FOUR-SIDED SQUARE BOX WOULD NEED ONLY TWO TEMPLATES: ONE FOR THE TOP AND ONE FOR THE SIDES. HOWEVER, IF YOU WOULD LIKE EACH SIDE TO BE DIFFERENT, YOU WILL NEED A TEMPLATE FOR EACH SIDE IN ADDITION TO ONE FOR THE TOP.

DEVELOP THUMBNAILS

Spread out your reference material in front of you. Include any design notes as well. Indicate which motifs you would like to include in your design. For example, from these two photos, my list might be:

- cottage

- tree

- lady in red

- picket fence

- curved path

- flower border

Make a series of sketches approximately 2" x 4" (5 cm x 10cm) that very roughly place the design elements. These are called *thumbnails*. Sketch the main elements first, then the supporting elements. There should be no detail. The goal is not to draw but to place each element most effectively.

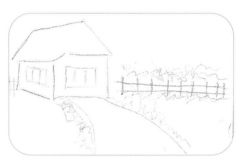

Here is a series of thumbnails based on the photographs at left.

MAKING A FINAL DECISION

Most of the time, one of your choices will stand out as obviously the best. If this is not the case, try these tie breakers:

• Review "What Makes a Good Composition?" (see pages 37-41). Does your design meet the requirements? If not, determine which elements need work and develop a few additional thumbnails.

• Check the proportions of the elements. Are they accurate? Are roses, for example, bigger than violets? Are elephants bigger than kittens?

• Do a few new thumbnails leaving out some of the elements in each. Sometimes a composition doesn't work because it's too crowded.

• Redo the thumbnails in questions in a larger format, approximately 4" x 6" (10cm x 15cm). Include more detail.

CHAPTER SEVEN

Step 5: Drawing

Perhaps no word strikes more fear in the heart of would-be designers than drawing. Unfortunately, it has kept many away from their dreams of designing. I feel so sad about this, especially since drawing is a completely learned skill and not nearly so difficult as some believe it to be.

The secret to drawing skill is practice. No one expects to sit down at a piano for the first time and play a beautiful sonata. Yet, many expect to be able to draw instantly. If they can't, they sigh deeply and say, "I just don't have the talent." Like playing a musical instrument, drawing is more about regular practice than talent. Even those born with an artistic or musical "gift" practice to develop it.

Keep a practice sketchbook just for you. No one else need see it, but please keep all your work. You will enjoy seeing your progress over time. If you diligently spend just thirty minutes per day drawing, you will see remarkable progress within a year. The subject matter you choose to draw is unimportant. What is important is daily consistency.

In the meantime, however, there are ways to legally "cheat." While you are getting started, these methods will provide quick results and build your confidence. But please don't rely on them exclusively for an indefinite period. Drawing without these aids will encourage versatility and many more choices.

DRAWING SHORTCUTS THAT GIVE GOOD RESULTS

Copyright-Free Artwork

Several companies publish compilations of copyright-free art, also known as *clip art*, including North Light Books and Dover Publications. Copyright-free art is typically published by subject, e.g., florals, holidays, Victorian and so forth. It is also available on the Internet and can be located by using a search engine and typing in *copyright-free art* or *clip art*. Please note that if the book or site does not clearly say the work is copyright-free, then it is not.

Copyright-free artwork is no longer subject to copyright protection due to its age. Some companies also publish designs that are produced specifically for the copyright-free market. You may use these in any design you choose without permission or fear of copyright violation. It's a good idea, however, to compile a design from several sources and not rely on a single piece of artwork for a pattern. This helps to ensure that no one else has a design that looks like yours.

TRACING

Simple Tracing

A fast way to produce a pattern is to trace a design from your own photograph. The photo must be your own; otherwise, the photographer's copyright is being violated.

Remember, however, that a camera foreshortens objects that are very close to the lens. If the photo looks distorted, the traced drawing will too.

TRACING, *continued*

Compound Tracing

Often a single photo does not contain all that is desired in a design. The solution is to combine several photos for a final pattern. Trace each element on a separate piece of tracing paper. Then, overlay the tracings to determine a final pattern. Some tracings may need to be enlarged or reduced on the photocopier so that the final drawing is in proportion.

In this example, I enlarged the leaves from the photo so that they would be in proportion to the rose.

Computer-Aided Tracing

Most computer painting or photo manipulation programs have a "sketch" option. The computer can make an outline drawing of selected motifs from either scanned or digital photographs. The resulting pattern may be a bit choppy, but the lines can be smoothed out by hand when tracing the final pattern.

Opaque Projector

While photos or their tracings can be reduced or enlarged via a photocopier, it can be inconvenient and time-consuming to interrupt your work for a trip to the copy store. Reductions and enlargements are also limited by the size of the copy paper and the copier. An opaque projector, which can enlarge or reduce on the spot is a versatile and convenient tool to have in an art studio or work area. A photo or other flat artwork is placed on the projector platform and then projected onto any surface. Simply adjust the image to the size you desire and trace for a pattern.

Opaque projectors are also ideal for mural painting. Draw your design to scale and project the final pattern onto the wall. This saves tons of time, and it's much easier and less awkward than drawing directly on the wall. To avoid distortion of the image, be sure the projector is perfectly perpendicular to the wall.

Opaque projectors are available in all price ranges. The more expensive projectors produce sharper images and offer a larger range of reduction and enlargement sizes.

A leader in the opaque projector market is Artograph (www.artograph.com). The company offers quality opaque projectors for every need and price range.

Michelle's Design Secrets

OPAQUE PROJECTORS ALSO PROVIDE A WONDERFUL SHORTCUT FOR PATTERN TRANSFER. INSTEAD OF USING TRANSFER PAPER, PROJECT THE IMAGE DIRECTLY ONTO A PREPARED PAINTING SURFACE, TRACE, AND YOU ARE READY TO PAINT.

Easy Steps to Drawing From Scratch

When you learn to play a musical instrument, you master scales and simple pieces before moving on to more complex arrangements. Drawing is much the same. Begin with something simple, such as a single flower, before attempting more complex flower arrangements.

An accurate drawing is very important. Beautiful color and fancy painting techniques will not hide a bad drawing—in fact, they often highlight the inadequacies. So, let's get started with some helpful tips on how to draw easily and accurately. I'll use a photograph of clematis as an example so you can see the steps in action.

Materials

- Tracing paper
- 4H pencil or
  lead holder with 4H lead
- Vinyl eraser
- Reference photo

Step One: Observe

This is the most important step. Careful observation results in more accurate drawings and a less frustrating experience. In this example, I will draw the two clematis blossoms in the foreground of the picture.

Look closely and note the details of the photo either mentally or on a piece of scrap paper. Here's my list for this photograph:

1 Round spiky centers.

2 Centers are about one-fourth the size of the flower.

3 Petals form an overall round shape.

4 Petals are oval-shaped with a pointed end.

5 Petals are smooth-edged.

6 Visual demarcation down the center of each petal.

7 Petals overlap as they grow.

8 Petals are joined to flower underneath the center. Attached end is not as pointy as free end.

9 Top flower has eight petals showing, while lower flower has seven.

10 If I draw a line horizontally through each flower, the top flower has five petals above the line and three below. The bottom flower has two completely above the line and half of a third. There are four and a half petals below the horizontal line. Repeat analysis with a vertical line.

11 Flowers in relation to one another: point of lowest petal of flower on right is one center's width below the flower on the left. Tip of middle-left petal on right flower just grazes top of center of flower on left.

Step Two: Mark the Boundaries

With light pencil marks, indicate the outermost boundaries of the top, bottom and sides of the subjects you will be drawing. This will ensure that you don't run out of paper! (This is a common occurrence for beginning artists.) Lightly indicate the placement of the most dominant features of the subject. In our example, this would be the petals and centers.

After the markings are indicated, do a careful check against your reference photo and observation notes. Are the proportions correct? Are the elements aligned correctly? Since not too much time and effort has been invested in the drawing at this point, now is the best and easiest time to make corrections.

Step Three: Connect the Dots!

Make a contour (outline) drawing of your subject using the boundary marks as a guide. Look at the reference photograph frequently.

Step Four: Fill in the Details

Indicate the more detailed portions of the subject.

Step Five: Proofread

Take a careful look at your drawing and at the reference photo. Do they look similar? If not, analyze why. Is each element in proportion to the rest? Are the angles correct? Are the sizes of individual features accurate? Correct if needed.

THE FINAL PATTERN

Commercial artists often draw the different design elements that they will be using on separate pieces of tracing paper. This allows for easy testing of placement and quick-and-easy compositional changes. Borders, geometric and repeating elements are often easier to draw on graph vellum where the measuring is already done for you.

You may decide that one of your elements is too big or too small in proportion to the others. You may then redraw the element to the proper size, or use an opaque projector or photocopier to reduce or enlarge

Michelle's Design Secrets

Reducing or enlarging on a photocopier is often an expensive guessing game. A proportional wheel eliminates some of the guesswork. The proportional wheel calculates the percent reduction or enlargement needed to bring an image to a desired size. Proportional wheels can be purchased at art and office supply stores.

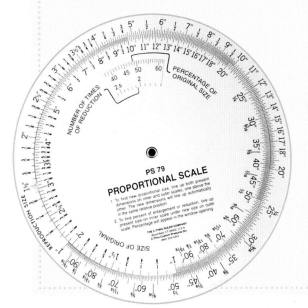

Michelle's Design Secrets

• Drawings should be clear and clean to ensure a well-defined pattern. Always keep your pencil sharp. Draw strong, definitive lines. Sketchy or overlapping lines result in hard-to-read patterns.

• Press lightly. Don't dig into the paper.

• Use a piece of tracing paper significantly larger than your drawing. This will leave room for any additions deemed necessary to ensure a better composition or to more adequately fit the surface. This also allows for the inevitable wear and tear at the edges of the paper.

• Draw similar elements the quick-and-easy way by simply turning the tracing paper to the reverse side. You now have double the number of flowers, leaves or whatever, but they look completely different now that the image is reversed. This is one of the many benefits of designing on tracing paper.

• Always label the top of the working pattern with the word *Top*. The orientation of floral patterns, in particular, is easily confused.

• Save all your drawings, even those not used in the final pattern. Chances are you can save design time by reusing portions in another pattern.

• Don't be worried or nervous if it takes longer than you'd like to draw the pattern. It almost always takes longer than you'd expect!

CHAPTER EIGHT

Step 6: Developing a Color Scheme

When I was a little girl we had a black-and-white television with a "rabbit ears" antenna to adjust the haphazard picture quality. Each April one of the major networks would air The Wizard of Oz. I sat glued to the television, immersed in a wonderment of song, dance and fantasy. One day twenty years later, while I was visiting a friend, The Wizard of Oz once again appeared on the television screen. We tuned in just as Dorothy's house went whirling into the tornado. Boom. The house landed in Oz. My eyes grew wide. Shock! Astonishment! Oz was in color! The difference in mood and effect was startling, dramatic and unforgettable.

Color has the power to change your design from forgettable to fabulous. In fact, research continually shows that it's the very first thing people notice about a design, ranking ahead of shape, style and motif. Choosing a color scheme does not have to be a matter of luck and guesswork. There are several proven methods that will make your piece sing.

THE COLOR WHEEL MAKES IT EASY

At your local art or craft store, purchase a color wheel. Here's an excellent one from Winsor & Newton that even includes a color mixing guide right on the wheel.

Color Wheel

PROPERTIES OF COLOR & COLOR SCHEMES

Colors depicted on a color wheel are shown in their richest, most vivid and intense versions. For example, red is on the color wheel, but its lighter and gentler self, pink, is not. Neither is burgundy, its deeper and darker self.

The purest, most intense form of a color is known as its *hue*. Your color scheme may be based on any version of this hue, including lighter versions called *tints* (the color plus white), darker versions called *shades* (the color plus black), or more neutralized, muted versions that are referred to as being less *intense*.

Value refers to the lightness or darkness of a color. For example, pink is a light value of red, while burgundy is a dark value. *Temperature* refers to the coolness or warmth of a color. Cool colors contain more blue, while warm colors contain more yellow.

Beautiful color combinations are guaranteed when any of the following color schemes are chosen from the color wheel.

Monochromatic

Mono means *one* and *chroma* means *color*. Therefore, this is simply a color scheme that uses several versions of one color that vary by value.

Analogous

Analogous color schemes use three to five colors that are next to each other on the color wheel.

A monochromatic green color scheme.

An analogous color scheme with yellow, orange and red.

Complementary

Complementary colors are those that are directly opposite each other on the color wheel. The most commonly used combinations are red and green, yellow and purple, and blue and orange.

Many beginning designers shy away from complementary color schemes because they think of red and green as just for Christmas, or yellow and purple as too much like Easter. This attitude is so limiting! The examples below show how effective a yellow-and-purple color scheme can be the whole year 'round. Notice also the variety in the blue-and-orange color schemes.

COLOR SCHEMES, *continued*

Split Complementary

A split complement uses three analogous colors plus the color directly opposite the middle of the three colors. You may also use just the two outer analogous colors plus the complement of the missing middle color.

Split complementary color schemes offer a pleasing blend of harmonious hues and dramatic accents.

Triadic

A triad uses three colors that are evenly spaced from each other on the wheel. It is among the most popular approaches to color selection. Its perfect balance makes it very pleasing to the eye.

Split Complementary

Triadic

ANOTHER FUN OPTION FOR CHOOSING COLOR SCHEMES

Here's yet another opportunity to use the reference material you have been so diligently clipping, photographing and filing. Pull out your Color reference file and select an image where the color just wows you. Below are some examples from my Color file.

Study the image you have selected and take note of its colors. Don't forget to include less obvious colors such as the background. They are part of what attracted you to the image.

For example, while my photo of the outdoor florist has beautiful flower colors, what really caught my attention were the colors reflected in the plastic wrapping.

Vintage Post Card, *circa* 1900

Vintage Post Card, *circa* 1930

Outdoor Florist

PAINT CHIP ORGANIZATION

Next, prepare paint swatches of the colors you see in the photo. Use scraps of watercolor paper about 1" by 1" (25mm x 25mm) or larger to create a set of paint chips. Premixed bottled colors such as FolkArt Acrylics by Plaid are easy to use.

In this example, you can see my reference photo and paint chips of colors based on the photo. Since the color scheme was pleasing in the photo, it will be pleasing in a design.

Michelle's Design Secrets

PAINT A CHIP OF EVERY COLOR YOU OWN ON A 1" BY 1" (25MM X 25MM) PIECE OF WATERCOLOR PAPER. STORE THESE IN SLIDE SHEETS FOR FAST AND EASY ORGANIZING. MAINTAIN A SEPARATE SET OF SLIDE SHEETS FOR EACH COLOR WHEEL HUE AND STORE THEM IN A BINDER. NOW, PAINT SWATCHES ARE ALWAYS READY AND AVAILABLE WHEN PLANNING COLOR SCHEMES. SLIDE SHEETS ARE INEXPENSIVE AND CAN BE PURCHASED AT PHOTOGRAPHY STORES. NOTE: SWATCH PAINTING GOES QUICKLY WHEN YOU USE DISPOSABLE COTTON SWABS INSTEAD OF A BRUSH TO PAINT THE COLOR ON THE CHIP.

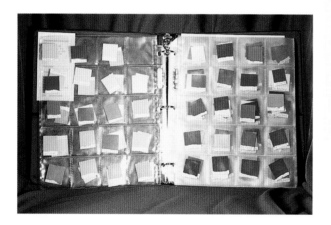

Indian corn and paint swatches

CREATING A MOOD

You may wish to create a specific mood for a piece. Perhaps you would like something exciting, or romantic, or maybe calming. Your choice of colors will have the greatest effect on setting a mood.

Take a look at the different moods of violet. When lightened it's peaceful, when darkened it's more intense, and at its pure hue it's active and exciting.

Cool colors are restful and peaceful.

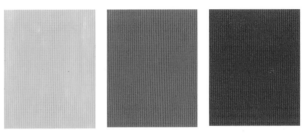

Warm colors are stimulating and exciting.

Light values and low intensities produce a calm and restful mood.

Dark values and higher intensities produce a stronger, more vibrant mood.

VALUE AND COLOR STUDIES

Once the color scheme has been selected, color place-ment is determined through value and color studies.

Each color in your selected palette needs a highlight and shadow. Select these colors from your color binder or mix them from scratch. A highlight is a color approximately two values lighter than the selected color. A shadow is approximately two values darker.

INDIAN CORN PALETTE

Here are the highlight and shadow colors from the Indian corn palette selected earlier. You may need several more values of each color. It's helpful to plan these now as well.

Value Studies

Using an HB pencil on a copy of the completed pattern, sketch in areas where you would like the light and dark values of your design. Keep the highlights and shadows consistent by imagining a light source at the top-right or -left corner of the design. This consistency will help give your painting depth and harmony. Complete at least three value studies, then choose the one that appeals to you most. Keep in mind that the center of interest should have the most value contrast of the design.

If your design needs more depth, lighten the light values or darken the darker values. Lighter values make objects appear to advance, while darker values make objects recede.

Color Studies

Using the colors from your planned palette, roughly paint in where you would like to place each color. Indicate highlights and shadows but don't spend time completing a careful painting. There is no need to load the brush for floating or other painting techniques; the goal here is to test color placement only. Do a few studies using different color placement. Each study should take no more than ten minutes.

Michelle's Design Secrets

SAVE TIME BY NOT RETRACING THE PATTERN FOR EACH VALUE STUDY. SIMPLY PLACE A PIECE OF TRACING PAPER OVER THE FINAL PATTERN AND COMPLETE THE VALUE STUDY RIGHT ON THE TRACING PAPER. ANOTHER TIME-SAVING OPTION IS TO REDUCE THE PATTERN ON A PHOTOCOPIER AND COMPLETE THE VALUE STUDY ON THE PHOTOCOPY.

YOU CAN SAVE TIME HERE AS WELL BY NOT TRACING YOUR PATTERN FOR EACH COLOR STUDY. PLACE A PIECE OF PREPARED ACETATE OVER THE PATTERN. YOU WILL BE ABLE TO SEE YOUR PATTERN RIGHT THROUGH THE ACETATE. PAINT THE COLOR STUDY RIGHT ON THE PREPARED ACETATE. THE SPECIAL COATING ALLOWS PAINT TO ADHERE TO THE SURFACE INSTEAD OF BEADING UP. WHEN THE PROJECT IS COMPLETED, THE PREPARED ACETATE CAN BE WIPED CLEAN WITH A WET PAPER TOWEL AND REUSED INDEFINITELY.

CHOOSING THE FINAL COLOR PLAN

Select the color study that appeals to you most using the following criteria: Is the color balanced throughout the design? Is there more contrast in hue or value at the center of interest? Are there enough highlights and shadows to create depth in each motif? Is there enough color variety in the piece? If one color is more dominant than the rest, is it in balance with the entire design?

If none of the color studies appeals to you, try a few more with some significant changes. For example: change the background color, add more highlights and shadows, or delete one of the colors with its corresponding highlight and shadow, etc.

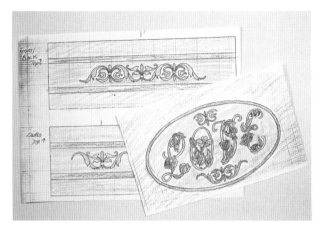

How to Make Colors Behave

How to make a color look lighter . . . . Place it next to a darker value

How to make a color look darker . . . . Place it next to a lighter value

How to make a color look warmer . . . . Place it next to something cooler

How to make a color look cooler . . . . Place it next to something warmer

How to make a color look brighter . . . . Place it next to its complement

How to make a color look duller . . . . Place it next to an analogous color

How to make a color come forward . . . . Make it warmer and/or lighter

How to make a color recede . . . . Make it cooler and/or darker

CHAPTER NINE

Step 7: Background Painting Techniques

At this point, you are almost ready to begin transferring the pattern to your painting surface. Just two more decisions must be made. First, you'll need to determine what kind of background would show off your design to its best advantage. Second, decide what technique you will use to paint your design.

Background Checks Required!

Both the color and the texture of the background have a dramatic effect on the look and feel of the piece.

Do you notice how the textured backgrounds below provide much more interest than the solid backgrounds? Decorative painting designs are almost always enhanced by textured rather than solid backgrounds.

Texture and Value

Textured backgrounds are achieved with a minimum of two colors. Two or three colors very close in *value* (the lightness or darkness of the *hue*) will result in a subtle background. Two or three colors far apart in value will result in a much more prominent background texture.

The same flower can look very different on different solid-colored backgrounds.

The same flower looks even more different when various textures are added to colored backgrounds.

(Background papers courtesy of Hot Off The Press, Inc.)

FAST AND FABULOUS BACKGROUND TECHNIQUES

Try these quick-and-easy techniques to add variety to your backgrounds.

Sponge Texture

This classic technique looks best when done with a lightly moistened natural sea sponge and a light touch.

Basecoat the piece in the desired color. It usually looks best if the basecoat is darker than the color used for sponging.

Wet the sponge thoroughly, then wring out as much water as possible. Wrap the sponge in a dry paper towel to wring out even more moisture.

Lightly dip the sponge in a puddle of the second paint color. Wipe the excess on a paper towel.

Lightly touch the loaded sponge to the surface, constantly turning your wrist so that no obvious patterns form. Reload as necessary.

If the sponge becomes soaked with paint, wring out the paint in the same manner that you wrung out the water.

Repeat with another color if desired.

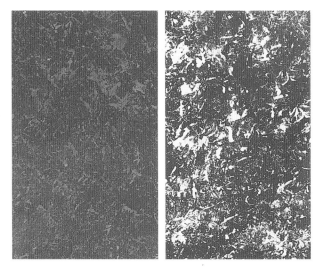

These two backgrounds were painted with the same technique, but notice the difference. The background on the left used two colors only one step apart on the value scale, while the background on the right used similar hues with more contrast in value.

Sponge Texture

Aluminum Foil Texture

This technique uses a crumpled ball of aluminum foil to pat on texture.

First, basecoat the piece in the desired color.

Dip a crumpled ball of aluminum foil into another color of paint.

Wipe the excess on a paper towel.

Repeatedly touch the foil ball to the surface and reload paint when necessary. When the foil becomes too clogged with paint, simply toss it out and start again with a fresh ball.

Repeat with another color if desired.

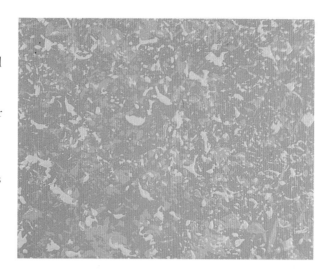

Plastic Wrap Texture, Technique I

Use a balled-up piece of plastic wrap in the same manner described above for the aluminum foil. The background of project three (page 110) in this book was painted using this technique.

Plastic Wrap Texture, Technique 2

The background of project two (page 94), "Heavenly Garden," was produced using one of my favorite techniques. The look is impressive but it is so quick and easy!

Using a ¾-inch flat brush, spread a thin coat of FolkArt Blending Gel over the painting surface and drop alternating blobs of selected paint colors onto the surface. Gather a handful of plastic wrap into a loose ball. Twist the plastic wrap down into the paint and lift. Repeat until the surface is blended. Allow to dry thoroughly.

Here's a sample of the same technique using a yellow color scheme.

Plastic Wrap Texture, Technique 3

Some materials are just so versatile! This technique also uses plastic wrap, but the results are completely different.

Basecoat the piece in the desired color. When it is dry, quickly paint on a second color. The second color should be at least two values darker or lighter than the basecoat. While this paint is still wet, lay a piece of plastic wrap directly onto the wet surface, covering it completely. Scrunch the plastic wrap slightly to create ridges.

When the paint is almost dry, lift the plastic wrap to reveal the completed background.

Michelle's Design Secrets

CREATE A VERY CONVINCING WATER EFFECT BY USING THIS TECHNIQUE WITH BLUES OR BLUE-GREENS. THE LOOK IS PERFECT FOR SEASCAPES OR NAUTICAL SCENES. PAINTED FISH LOOK RIGHT AT HOME!

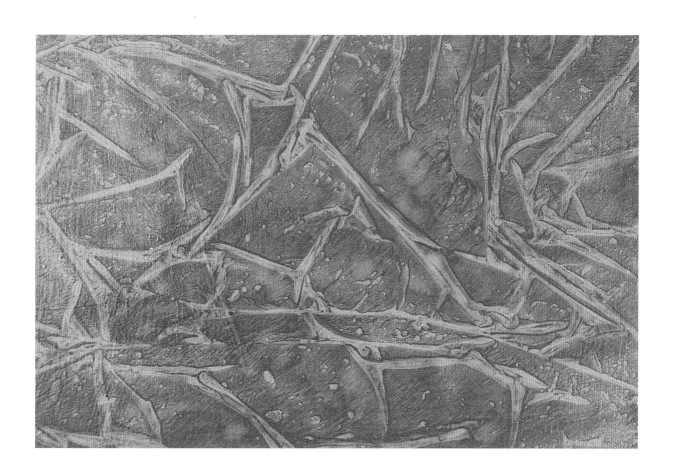

BRUSH TEXTURES

Deerfoot Stippler

With specialty brushes such as rakes and deerfoot stipplers you can create many different background effects.

Project one (page 82) from this book, "The Greatest of These is Love," uses a deerfoot stippler to achieve a soft mottled background.

Basecoat the piece in the desired color. Dip a deerfoot stippler in a second color that has been thinned to the consistency of heavy cream. Holding the brush over your piece, lightly run your thumb along the brush. Paint spatters will randomly spray over your piece, adding great textural effects. If your piece is large, you may want to do this outside, or protect your indoor work area with newspaper.

The deerfoot stippler can also be used as a spattering tool to create this interesting background texture.

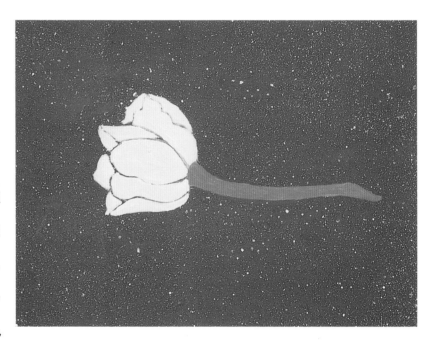

Michelle's Design Secrets

THIS IS A GREAT TECHNIQUE TO COMBINE WITH THE TECHNIQUE ON THE FOLLOWING PAGE IN ORDER TO CREATE AN AGED, ANTIQUE LOOK. RAKE THE BACKGROUND FIRST, THEN FINISH WITH LIGHT SPATTERING USING THE DEERFOOT STIPPLER.

Rake

This is the only time I will encourage you to abuse your brush!

While the rake is well-known for quickly creating hair and beards, it is also versatile enough to produce a fabulous background texture.

Basecoat the piece in the desired color.

Fully load the rake with your second color. On the palette, heavily bear down on the brush, bending the bristles so that they splay out at all angles. Lightly drag the prepared brush across the background.

Flat or Angle Brush

Here's an impressive background that is produced using only an angle brush, some blending gel and two or three paint colors.

This one is real quick—no basecoating needed! Coat the surface with a thin layer of blending gel. Randomly drip dime-size (18mm) blobs of paint onto the surface. Use two or three colors for best results. Simply pull the brush diagonally through the blobs of paint, working your way over the entire surface. Every few strokes, wipe excess paint from your brush onto a paper towel.

Michelle's Design Secrets

To make this technique look like marble, dip the chisel end of your brush into a light-value paint color and dab randomly onto the surface.

PLAY-DOH TECHNIQUES

Here's another super quick technique that doesn't require any basecoating.

Roll a small ball of Play-Doh into a log. It doesn't matter what color Play-Doh you use. Set it aside.

Randomly drip quarter-size (25mm) blobs of paint on your design surface. Use two or three colors for best results.

Roll your Play-Doh log through the paint. The colors will partially blend, resulting in a mottled texture that resembles natural stone. The look changes considerably depending on the colors you use.

Any others?

Yes, heaps! Just look around your kitchen or through your painting supplies. Almost anything can be used to create a texture. Try cheesecloth, textured fabric or crumpled paper. Your imagination is the limit!

Set aside some time one day soon to experiment. Use poster board as an inexpensive surface to try new techniques. Record the materials used and how you achieved the effect. And don't forget to include samples of your new techniques in your Decorative Painter's C.E.O.!

How to Choose the Best Background for a Design

Try two or three background techniques on a 6" x 6" (15cm x 15cm) piece of poster board. Refer to your color reference and color studies to choose paints.

Next, lay the chips from your chosen color palette on the background studies. Which background choice most enhances your chosen palette?

Make sure every color is clearly visible on the background you choose. Colors very close in value to the background may be difficult to see. For example, if you choose a green background for a floral painting, the green background will need to be lighter or darker, or warmer or cooler, than the leaves in your floral design so that they do not disappear into the background.

If choosing a background becomes difficult, try this: select a small section or motif from your main design that contains all or most of the colors that will be used in the final painting, then paint it on watercolor paper or poster board. Remember, you don't need a perfectly painted sample; a very rough one will do.

Cut out the painted sample and lay it on top of your test backgrounds. Choose the option that best enhances the design without overwhelming or competing with it. Also, consider the style of the surface. Is it contemporary? Traditional? Country? Choose the background texture that reflects the style of the surface.

Michelle's Design Secrets

IT IS HELPFUL TO BE ABLE TO COMPARE SEVERAL CHOICES AT ONCE, BUT REPAINTING THE TEST SECTION SEVERAL TIMES CAN BE VERY TIME-CONSUMING.

INSTEAD, PAINT THE MOTIF ONCE, THEN MAKE COLOR PHOTOCOPIES. PLACE THE MOTIF ON THE DIFFERENT BACKGROUNDS AND COMPARE.

THE LAST DECISION: DECORATIVE PAINTING TECHNIQUE

Right about now you are heading in to home plate. The crowd is cheering. Well, at least you are! Home is in sight and you are about to score a run, a beautiful ready-to-paint design! There is just one last stretch of ground to cover and that is to select a painting technique.

Many famous artists have memorable painting styles. Mention Monet or Renoir and we think *impressionist*. Mention Seurat and we think *pointillist*. Mention Grandma Moses and we think *primitive*. Each of these artists employed a specific technique to indicate form, shading, highlight, etc. Monet and Renoir used free-flowing brush strokes; Seurat used thousands of little dots. What technique will you use to paint your final design?

Once you have decided which technique you would like to use, try it out on a piece of watercolor paper or poster board prepared with the type of background you have chosen. Reproduce a portion of your design on this practice surface. This last study will allow you to accurately see how your design will look when painted on the actual surface. Fine tune your technique and make any other adjustments at this stage.

You are now ready to confidently paint your design on the final surface.

Floated Color

If you are an experienced decorative painter, this technique will be very familiar to you. Floated color results in a smooth transition between values and is accomplished by loading the brush with half paint and half water. The paint side is then brushed over the desired area, producing a smooth value change.

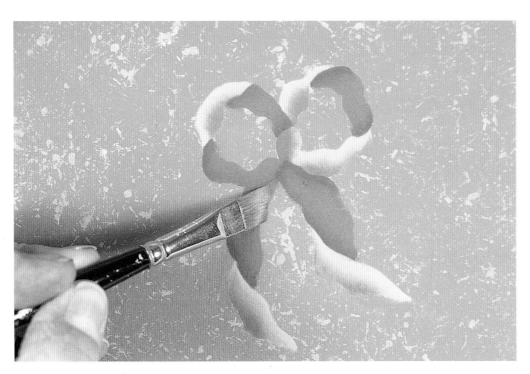

Floated Color

Beyond Floated Color: Other Painting Techniques

While most modern decorative painting is done with floated color, there are so many more techniques that can be used to highlight and shade. Why not take time now to learn some new ways? You will not only expand your painting skills; you will make your work that much more individual.

You'll learn these new skills while painting four popular garden flowers: pansy, lily, peony and anemone. Paint these on practice board or on the surface of your choice.

PALETTE

FolkArt Acrylics by Plaid

Amish Blue

Black Cherry

Bright Baby Pink

Buttercream

Buttercup

Dark Pink mix (Fuchsia to Hauser Green Medium 5:1)

Dark Plum

Fuchsia

Glazed Carrots

Hauser Green Dark

Hauser Green Light

Hauser Green Medium

Licorice

Light Fuchsia

Lime Yellow

Medium Orange

Medium Pink mix (Light Fuchsia to Hauser Green Medium 5:1)

Purple Lilac

Sky Blue

Sunflower

BRUSHES

Loew-Cornell

Series 7000 no. 4 round

Series 7550 1½-inch (36mm) wash

La Corneille
JS-2 Jackie Shaw liner no. 2

Unless otherwise noted, all painting is done with a no. 4 round.

PANSY: WATER BLENDING

First, basecoat each area and allow it to dry. Then, before each highlight or shadow is added, dampen the surface with clean water. Use enough water to create a shine but not enough to form puddles. Place the highlight or shadow color directly on the damp surface.

The pigment will immediately disperse, leaving a soft blend. Any harsh lines can be blended out with a damp brush. For smooth value transitions, two to three layers of paint may be needed.

1 Basecoat the leaves and stems using Hauser Green Light. Shade with Hauser Green Medium, and shade again with Hauser Green Dark. Highlight with Lime Yellow.

2 Basecoat the pansy petals with Amish Blue, Purple Lilac, Medium Pink, and Glazed Carrots. Shade the Amish Blue petals with Dark Plum and highlight with Sky Blue. Shade the Purple Lilac petals with Dark Plum and highlight with Sky Blue, except for the front-most Purple Lilac pansy, which is highlighted with Bright Baby Pink. Shade the Medium Pink petals with Dark Plum and highlight with Bright Baby Pink. Shade the Glazed Carrot petals with Black Cherry and highlight with Medium Orange. Basecoat the centers with Buttercup and shade with Glazed Carrots. Paint the white stripes with Buttercream.

3 Use the JS-2 liner with Licorice to draw in the black markings. Do not dampen the surface first, and do not blend them into the other colors.

LILY: BRUSH BLENDING

The secret to this technique is the paint consistency, which must be like thick, heavy cream. Too little water will make the paint drag rather than blend. Too much water will cause the paint to run. A Masterson Sta-Wet palette is the key to keeping your paint at the proper consistency. Basecoat each area and allow it to dry. Then lightly basecoat the area again and place the shadows and highlights in the desired areas. Using the brush at a low angle, and with a light touch, blend the values together. Two to three coats will develop the most depth. Allow each coat to dry before adding the next.

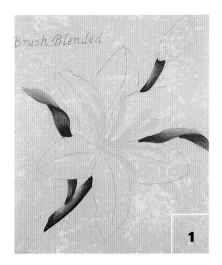

1 Basecoat the leaves and stems with Hauser Green Light, shade with Hauser Green Medium, and shade again with Hauser Green Dark. Highlight with Lime Yellow. Basecoat the pistils and stamens with Lime Yellow.

2 Basecoat the petals with Buttercup, shade with Glazed Carrots. Wash the pistils and stamens with Buttercup.

3 Shade the petals again with Medium Pink and highlight with Buttercream. Basecoat the stamens with Glazed Carrots and shade with Medium Pink.

4 Add accents of Black Cherry in the darkest shaded areas. Add dash markings on the petals with Black Cherry.

PEONY: DRYBRUSHING

Once the basecoating is completed, set aside your water container. The secret to this technique is to use as little water as possible. Do not rinse your brush when changing colors. Wipe your brush clean on a dry paper towel between colors instead. To paint, load your brush with the shadow or highlight color and then wipe the excess on a dry paper towel. Move the brush lightly over the surface to deposit the color. Several coats will be needed to build depth.

1 Basecoat the leaves and stems with Hauser Green Light. Shade with Hauser Green Medium and then Hauser Green Dark.

2 Highlight the leaves and stems with Lime Yellow.

3 Working one petal at a time, basecoat the petals with Medium Pink, then shade with Dark Pink.

4 Reinforce the shading with Black Cherry. Highlight the petals with Bright Baby Pink. Highlight the tips of the petals with Sunflower.

ANEMONE: UNBLENDED

This technique goes quickly, so it is very rewarding. One coat of shading and highlighting often is all that is needed. After the basecoat is dry, add shadows and highlights simply by painting fine, tightly spaced overlapping lines. The secret to this technique is that the lines must be painted following the shape of the object. For example, petal shading must curve and bend with the petal.

1 Basecoat the leaves with Hauser Green Light. Basecoat the orange anemone with Glazed Carrots; shade with Medium Pink. Basecoat the blue anemone with Amish Blue, shade with Dark Plum. Basecoat the centers with Licorice.

2 Deepen the shading on the orange anemone with Black Cherry, then highlight with Medium Orange. Deepen the shading on the blue anemone with Licorice, and highlight with Sky Blue. Dot the centers with Dark Plum.

3 Add highlights to both anemones with Buttercream.

4 Shade the leaves with Hauser Green Medium and then again with Hauser Green Dark. Highlight with Lime Yellow.

Putting Your Design Skills to Work on Painted Projects

Pencil. Paint. Brushes. Action! The following three projects reveal the seven-step design process from the spark of an idea to the finished project. Note the unique development of each design. It doesn't happen all at once, but rather unfolds step by step.

If you need a shot of confidence before you begin to create your own designs, paint along with me. Pay special attention to the seven steps in action as you paint. Notice how each project is remarkably different, yet each uses the process as a foundation and as a springboard.

After completing these projects, put your newly-developed design skills, together with your imagination and creativity, to work. Begin creating your own painted pieces that are beautiful, original and uniquely you.

The Greatest of These is Love

The classic box is one of decorative painting's most popular and versatile surfaces. Useful in any room—and a much appreciated gift—boxes take on new significance when they are beautiful as well as functional.

For a designer, the sides and top of a box offer opportunities for learning as well as space for an endless variety of design options. Mastery of the box shape also will prepare you for larger scale projects. Furniture is often built in the shape of a box: chests, dressers, nightstands, wardrobes and cabinets. Even the walls, floor and ceiling of a room form a box.

This project teaches several design strategies to use on boxlike shapes. Notice

that the colors used on the top, the design's center of interest, are repeated on the sides of the box. This unifies the design even though the painting is on several different planes. Notice also that the borders on the sides of the box are taken directly from the main design, again providing continuity and harmony. To add interest and rhythm, the side motif was created by elongating the border. Its colors are different from those found in the motif on the top of the box, although these colors are repeated elsewhere in the main design. The feminine color scheme is complemented by the equally feminine style of the lettering and floral motifs.

PATTERN

This pattern may be
hand-traced or photocopied
for personal use only.
Enlarge at 200%

©2002 BMS, Inc

This pattern may
be hand-traced or
photocopied for
personal use only.

This pattern may be
hand-traced or photocopied
for personal use only.
Enlarge at 200%.

©2002 BMS, Inc

COLORS & MATERIALS

PAINT: FOLKART ACRYLICS BY PLAID

BABY BLUE

BALLET PINK

BUTTERCREAM

DARK SALMON

FRENCH BLUE

HAUSER GREEN DARK

HAUSER GREEN LIGHT

HAUSER GREEN MEDIUM

LAVENDER

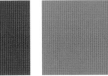

LIGHT FUCHSIA

LIGHT ROSE PINK MIX
(BALLET PINK TO ROSE
PINK 2:1)

LIME YELLOW

RASPBERRY SHERBET

ROSE PINK

STERLING BLUE

SUNFLOWER

TURNER'S YELLOW

VIOLET PANSY

SURFACE

Miniature Lane Cedar Chest

Available from
Bella Michelle Studios, Inc.

michelle@bellamichelle.com

BRUSHES: LOEW-CORNELL

La Corneille Series 7150
¾-inch (20mm) flat

Series 410
¼-inch (6mm) deerfoot stippler

La Corneille Series 7350
liner no. 2

La Corneille
JS-2 Jackie Shaw mid-length
liner no. 2

ADDITIONAL SUPPLIES

Loew-Cornell transfer paper

Masterson Sta-Wet palette

FolkArt Artists' Varnish Matte

PLANNING THE DESIGN

1 For my reference piece, I used one of my own watercolor sketches.

2 I chose to build the color scheme around a classic red, yellow and blue triad. I selected samples of FolkArt colors from my swatch book that will provide a light, medium and dark value of each hue.

3 For the pattern, I moved the letters closer together to better fit the proportions of the box. I also enclosed the *love* sentiment in an oval to give the design a cozier feel.

The design on top looks nice, but a bit empty. Time to try some alternate layouts. In the bottom version, I pulled motifs from the side of the box and added them to the inside of the oval. This improved the design by adding emphasis to my center of interest as well as unifying the top of the box with the sides.

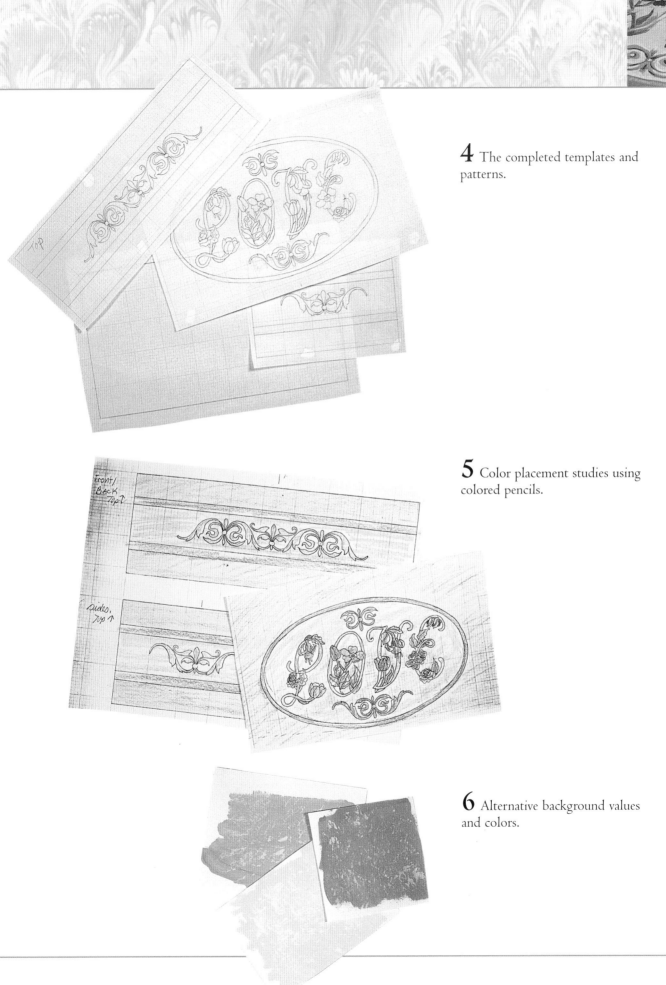

4 The completed templates and patterns.

5 Color placement studies using colored pencils.

6 Alternative background values and colors.

PAINTING THE PROJECT

7 Cover the hinges on the back of the box with tape to protect them from paint.

    With the ¾-inch (20mm) flat brush, basecoat the oval with Sunflower and the area surrounding the oval with Rose Pink.

    With the deerfoot stippler, stipple the oval with Buttercream and the area surrounding the oval with Light Rose Pink.

8 Using the no. 2 liner, basecoat the sides of the box: Use Rose Pink for the top and bottom stripes, Sunflower for the center stripe, and French Blue for the blue stripe separating the pink and yellow.

    Using the deerfoot stippler, stipple the pink stripes with Light Rose Pink, the center stripe with Buttercream, and the blue stripes with Baby Blue.

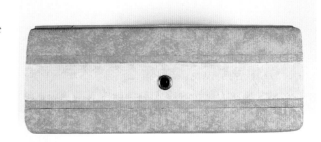

9 Transfer the remaining details of the pattern to the top and sides.

SCROLLWORK

10 Using the no. 2 liner, basecoat the scrollwork on the sides of the box with Light Rose Pink. Shade by outlining the bottom of the scrollwork with Rose Pink.

11 Highlight by outlining the top of the scrollwork with Ballet Pink.

12 Deepen the shading with Rose Pink.

    With the JS-2 liner, paint a thin line of Sterling Blue along the edge of the blue stripe that meets the yellow stripe.

13 To accent the scrollwork, paint random lines of Sterling Blue under the Rose Pink.

14 Using the no. 2 liner, basecoat the border of the oval and the scrollwork with French Blue, the lettering with Light Rose Pink, and the stems and leaves with Hauser Green Light.

15 With the tip of the no. 2 liner, paint random dots of Baby Blue on the oval border.

Using the JS-2 liner, paint a thin line of Sterling Blue on each side of the blue oval border.

Shade the scrollwork by outlining the bottom with Sterling Blue. Highlight by outlining the top of the scrollwork with Baby Blue.

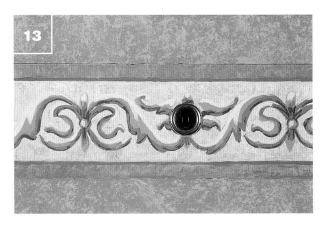

Note: For all of the following steps, use the no. 2 liner.

16 Shade the *L* and the *O* with Rose Pink.

Basecoat the bowl of the fuchsia with Light Fuchsia, the petals with Lavender and the pistils and stamens with Turner's Yellow.

Basecoat the rose with Dark Salmon.

Basecoat the tulips with French Blue. Basecoat the inner petals with Sterling Blue.

Basecoat the center of the poppy with Turner's Yellow and the petals with Dark Salmon.

17 Deepen the shading on the *L* and the *O* with Raspberry Sherbet.

Shade the bowl of the fuchsia with Raspberry Sherbet, the petals with Violet Pansy and the pistils and stamens with Dark Salmon.

Shade the rose with Raspberry Sherbet.

Shade the tulip on the *L* with Sterling Blue, the inner petals of the tulip on the *O* with Violet Pansy and the outer petals with Sterling Blue.

Shade the bottom and left side of the leaves and stems with Hauser Green Medium.

18 Highlight the *L* and the *O* with Ballet Pink.

Highlight the bowl and the petals of the fuchsia with Ballet Pink.

Highlight the tulips with Baby Blue and then Ballet Pink.

Highlight the poppy with Rose Pink and then Ballet Pink.

Highlight the leaves and stems with Lime Yellow.

19 Shade the *V* and the *E* with Rose Pink.
Basecoat the front petals of the tulips with French Blue and the back petals with Sterling Blue.
Basecoat the bowl of the fuchsia with Light Fuchsia and the petals with Lavender.
Basecoat the poppy hiding under the top of the *E* with French Blue. Basecoat the poppy in the center of the E with Dark Salmon, with a center of Turner's Yellow.
Basecoat the rose with Light Fuchsia.
Basecoat the leaves and the stems with Hauser Green Light, except for the inside of the tulip leaf, which is basecoated with Hauser Green Dark.

20 Deepen the shading of the *V* and the *E* with Raspberry Sherbet.
Shade the bowl of the fuchsia with Raspberry Sherbet and the petals with Violet Pansy.
Shade the tulip with Sterling Blue.
Shade the petals and the center of the middle poppy with Raspberry Sherbet.
Shade the rose with Raspberry Sherbet.
Shade the leaves and stems with Hauser Green Medium.

21 Highlight the *V* and the *E* with Ballet Pink.
Highlight the tulip with Baby Blue and then with Ballet Pink.
Highlight the fuchsia petals and the bowl with Ballet Pink.
Highlight the petals of the blue poppy with Baby Blue and then with Ballet Pink. Highlight the petals of the red poppy with Ballet Pink.
Highlight the rose with Ballet Pink.
Highlight the leaves and the stems with Lime Yellow.
To accent the scrollwork, paint random lines of Raspberry Sherbet under the Sterling Blue.

22 The completed oval.

Heavenly Garden

This is a perfect piece to paint on a dreary winter day to bring the sunshine and flowers of spring into your home a bit early. The cloudlike background suggests a view of heaven through the beauty of the natural world.

With its analogous cool color scheme, this piece provides a feeling of tranquility. Its brightly toned hue adds optimism to the mood as well. To reinforce the center of interest and to add harmony to the whole, the yellow of the forget-me-not centers is repeated in accents on the center roses.

The piece incorporates a "border violation," which is one of my favorite design strategies. It sounds dangerous, but it's not! In fact, it's one of the most successful ways to add interest and variety to a design. "Border violation" simply means to extend the design beyond the obvious boundaries of a piece. The design for Heavenly Garden could have been contained completely in the center of the tray, but look how much more interesting the design is when it extends beyond its primary space and into the frame of the tray. Look for this design strategy in project three, Romance, also.

PATTERN

This pattern may be hand-traced
or photocopied for personal use only.
Enlarge at 111% to bring it up to
full size.

COLORS & MATERIALS

PAINT: FolkArt by Plaid

AZURE BLUE   BABY BLUE   BABY PINK   BUTTERCUP

DARK PINK
(FUCHSIA:MYSTIC
GREEN 6:1)   LAVENDER   LIGHT LAVENDER
(WICKER WHITE:
LAVENDER 4:1)   LIGHT PERIWINKLE

MEDIUM PINK
(LIGHT FUCHSIA:MYSTIC
GREEN 6:1)   MYSTIC GREEN   PERIWINKLE   RED VIOLET

ROBIN'S EGG BLUE
(WICKER WHITE:SKY
BLUE:AZURE BLUE 4:2:1)   ROBIN'S EGG BLUE LIGHT
(WICKER WHITE:SKY
BLUE:AZURE BLUE 5:2:1)   SHAMROCK   SKY BLUE

SPRING GREEN   WICKER WHITE   YELLOW OCHRE

SURFACE

12" x 16" (19cm x 38cm) Chippendale Tray by Walnut Hollow.

Available at art and craft stores nationwide. Also available from:

Walnut Hollow Farm, Inc.
1409 State Road 23
Dodgeville, WI 53533
(800) 950-5101
www.walnuthollow.com

BRUSHES: LOEW-CORNELL

La Corneille series 7150
¾" (18mm) flat

La Corneille series 7000
round no. 4

ADDITIONAL SUPPLIES

Wood sealer

Loew-Cornell transfer paper

FolkArt Blending Gel

Masterson Art Products
plastic solvent cups

Masterson Sta-Wet palette

Plastic wrap

FolkArt Artists' Varnish Matte

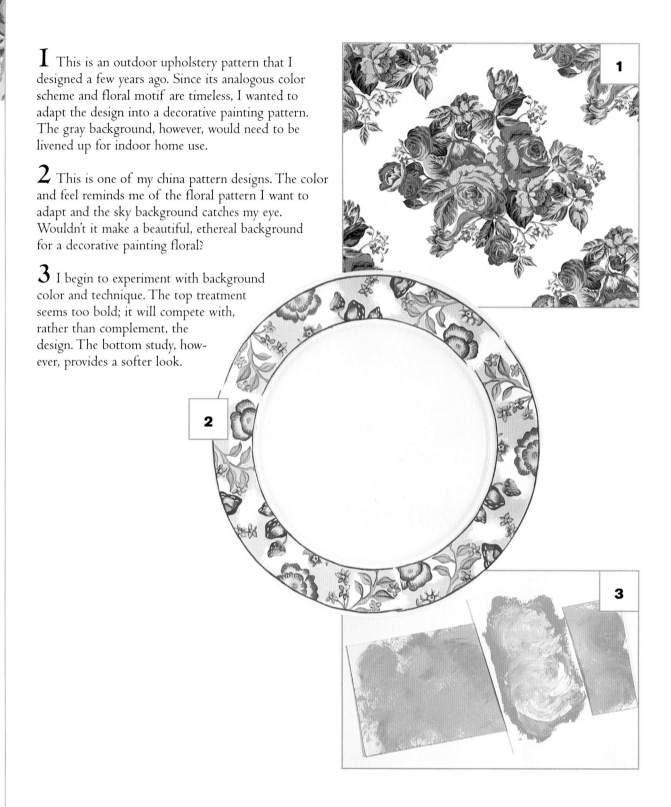

1 This is an outdoor upholstery pattern that I designed a few years ago. Since its analogous color scheme and floral motif are timeless, I wanted to adapt the design into a decorative painting pattern. The gray background, however, would need to be livened up for indoor home use.

2 This is one of my china pattern designs. The color and feel reminds me of the floral pattern I want to adapt and the sky background catches my eye. Wouldn't it make a beautiful, ethereal background for a decorative painting floral?

3 I begin to experiment with background color and technique. The top treatment seems too bold; it will compete with, rather than complement, the design. The bottom study, however, provides a softer look.

4 Here I test my colors on a sample of the chosen background to ensure that values and intensities do not disappear into the background.

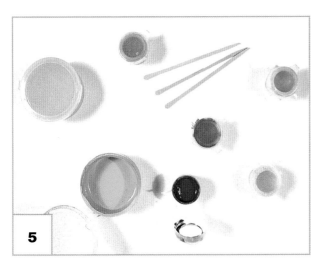

5 Not all the colors I want are available in premixed bottle acrylics. However, I can easily mix whatever I need. To save time and eliminate the need for remixing, I store mixed colors in plastic solvent cups from Masterson Art Products, Inc.

6 The original pattern, while appropriate for a large-scale upholstery pattern, is too busy for the smaller-scale tray I chose for a surface. When I redrew the pattern, I left out some of the secondary flowers but added a butterfly to the design for movement and interest.

To ensure that my color placement was balanced, I did a colored pencil color placement study on a copy of the final pattern.

Michelle's Design Secrets

WHEN DESIGNING FLORALS, I FIND IT HELPFUL TO INDICATE THE LEAF COLORS FIRST IN COLORED PENCIL AND THEN PLAN THE COLORS OF THE FLOWERS. THE GREENS OF THE LEAVES ARE USUALLY REPEATED THROUGHOUT A FLORAL DESIGN, SO INDICATING THOSE FIRST MAKES IT EASIER TO BALANCE THE COLORS OF THE FLOWERS.

7 Seal the tray using the sealer of your choice. Sand until smooth. Using the ¾-inch (18mm) flat brush, spread a thin coat of blending gel over the surface of the tray. Drop alternating random blobs of Robin's Egg Blue Light and Robin's Egg Blue onto the tray surface. Gather a handful of plastic wrap into a loose ball. Twist the plastic wrap down into the paint and lift. Repeat until the paint is evenly blended across the surface. Allow to dry thoroughly.

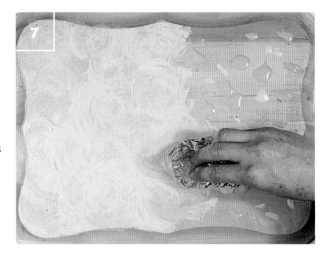

8 Don't overblend. Let the swirls remain so the texture looks uneven.

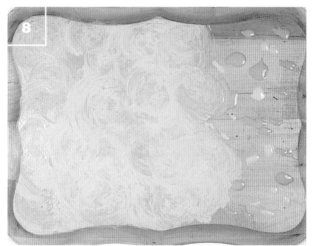

9 Basecoat the center of the forget-me-nots with Buttercup. Add a dot of Yellow Ochre to the middle of each center.

  Basecoat the flower stems and leaves with Mystic Green. Highlight with Spring Green on the left side of the stems and leaves. Shade the right side of the stems with Shamrock and the right side and bottom of the

Forget-Me-Nots

10 Close-up of leaves.

11 Basecoat the forget-me-nots with Light Periwinkle. Shade the left side of the petals with Periwinkle.

12 Highlight the right side of the petals with Baby Blue.

13 Basecoat the first tulip with Light Periwinkle. Shade with Periwinkle.

14 Deepen the shading with Red Violet. Highlight with Baby Blue.

15 Paint the second tulip in the same manner.

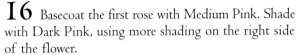

16 Basecoat the first rose with Medium Pink. Shade with Dark Pink, using more shading on the right side of the flower.

17 Highlight the rose with Baby Pink, highlighting more heavily on the left side of the flower.

18 Deepen the shading on the right side of the rose with Red Violet.

19 Basecoat the first peony with Lavender. Shade with Red Violet.

20 Highlight the peony with Light Lavender, then with Baby Pink, highlighting more heavily on the right side of the flower. Deepen the shading with Red Violet.

21 Basecoat the second peony with Medium Pink. Shade with Lavender.

22 Highlight with Baby Pink, highlighting more heavily on the right side of the flower. Deepen the shading with Red Violet.

23 Basecoat the second rose with Medium Pink. Shade with Dark Pink.

24 Highlight with Light Pink and accent with Buttercup.

THIRD TULIP

25 Basecoat the third tulip with Medium Pink. Shade with Lavender, then highlight with Light Pink.

26 Deepen the shading with Periwinkle.

THIRD PEONY

27 Basecoat the third peony with Lavender. Shade with Periwinkle.

28 Highlight with Light Lavender and then Baby Pink. Deepen the shading with Red Violet.

29 Basecoat the fourth tulip with Medium Pink. Shade with Dark Pink, then highlight with Baby Pink.

BUTTERFLY

30 Basecoat the butterfly's body and antenna with Red Violet. Basecoat the ruffles with Lavender. Basecoat the stripes and dots with Buttercup. Basecoat the wings with Light Periwinkle.

31 Shade the ruffle with Red Violet. Shade the stripes and dots with Yellow Ochre and highlight with Wicker White. Shade the wings with Periwinkle.

32 Highlight the ruffle with Light Lavender and the wings with Baby Blue.

ADD ACCENTS

33 Use Buttercup and Wicker White to add accents to the flowers at the center of interest (the first two roses and the first tulip). Mix a little Buttercup and Spring Green on your palette to add accents to the tips of the leaves.

34 Add small accents of Dark Pink to the base of the leaves.

Varnish with FolkArt Artists' Varnish Matte.

Romance

If you'd like more romance in your life, consider adding this piece to your home. Become lost in the memory of a former or current love as you paint the timeless symbols of romance: A full heart, an eager cupid, a red rose for love, a yellow rose for loyalty, pansies for remembrance, bluebells for constancy and a lady's fan for femininity.

The designer in you should note the classic red, yellow and blue triadic color scheme in the center oval, enhanced by the red and green complementary color scheme of the background.

Notice how the frame of the oval appears shiny and metallic even though no metallic paints were used. The secret lies in the careful use of contrasting values. The lightest and brightest highlights were used sparingly to make the oval appear to glow. The only other place these pale yellow highlights appear is on the yellow rose, making it stand out as the center of interest.

Also, as in the Heavenly Garden project, the center design extends beyond its main boundaries to add visual interest to the piece.

PATTERN

This pattern may be hand-traced or photocopied for personal use only. Enlarge at 110% to bring it up to full size.

COLORS & MATERIALS

PAINT: FOLKART BY PLAID

BABY BLUE

BALLET PINK

BASIL GREEN

CHRISTMAS RED

DARK PEACH PERFECTION mix (PEACH PERFECTION to NUTMEG 4:1)

DARK YELLOW mix (SUNNY YELLOW to YELLOW OCHRE 5:1)

FRENCH BLUE

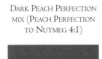
HAUSER GREEN LIGHT

HAUSER GREEN MEDIUM

HOLIDAY RED

LEMONADE

LIME LIGHT

MEDIUM YELLOW mix (SUNNY YELLOW to YELLOW OCHRE 6:1)

NUTMEG

PEACH PERFECTION

POPPY RED

PURPLE LILAC

SHAMROCK

SKINTONE

STERLING BLUE

SUNNY YELLOW

TRUE BURGUNDY

WICKER WHITE

YELLOW OCHRE

SURFACE

Upright Secretary, available from:

Viking Woodcrafts, Inc.
1317 8th St. SE
Waseca, MN 56093
(800) 328-0116
www.vikingwoodcrafts.com

BRUSHES: LOEW-CORNELL

Series 790
1-inch (25mm) oval wash

Series 410
¼-inch (6mm) deerfoot stippler

La Corneille series 7120
⅛-inch (3mm) rake

La Corneille
JS-2 Jackie Shaw liner no. 2

La Corneille series 7000
round no. 4

ADDITIONAL SUPPLIES

Wood sealer

Loew-Cornell transfer paper

Masterson Art Products plastic solvent cups

Masterson Sta-Wet palette

Plastic wrap

FolkArt Artists' Varnish Matte

Two ¾-inch (18mm) gold-tone knobs (purchase at a hardware or cabinetry store)

PLANNING THE DESIGN

1 Sometimes it is fun to use various references from the Inspiration section of your Decorative Painter's C.E.O. and combine them into one design. Here are several references from my own files that I used to create this project.

2 These are some rough thumbnail sketches I made to test compositional options. Don't worry about your drawing—notice that these sketches are probably unreadable for anyone but me. You are the only one who needs to see and interpret your thumbnails.

3 My final design included separate patterns for both the foreground and the background because I wanted the main design to appear like a picture hanging against patterned wallpaper. Color and value would be critical to achieving such an illusion, so I completed several value studies to help me determine where to place areas of contrast and establish a center of interest.

Michelle's Design Secrets

SAVE TIME BY REDUCING YOUR PATTERN ON A PHOTO-COPIER FOR VALUE AND COLOR STUDIES. A FULL-SIZE PATTERN IS NOT NECESSARY FOR THIS STEP, AND MAKING ONE WILL ONLY SLOW YOU DOWN.

4 For a color study, I lay a piece of prepared acetate over a reduced photocopy of my pattern.

5 Sometimes I complete more than one study before I make a choice. In this case I wanted to see more options before choosing a final color scheme, so I transferred the design at full size to a sheet of watercolor paper. Here you can see all the options I tried. Notice how different the backgrounds look, even though they are all variations of a red and green complementary color scheme. There is tremendous variety in the color wheel!

PAINTING THE DESIGN

Unless otherwise noted, the no. 4 round brush is used for all painting.

6 Seal the wood piece using the sealer of your choice. Sand until smooth.

Using the 1-inch (25mm) oval wash brush and Holiday Red paint, basecoat all surfaces of the piece except the oval on the cabinet front. Allow to dry.

Crunch up a piece of plastic wrap and dip it into a puddle of Christmas Red. Wipe the excess on a paper towel. Tap the ball lightly over all the Holiday Red surfaces, constantly turning your wrist to avoid a regular pattern.

7 Close-up view of finished background.

8 Basecoat the area surrounding the ribbon with Shamrock. Using a ¼-inch (6mm) deerfoot stippler, stipple the area with Hauser Green Medium.

9 Shade the ribbon with True Burgundy, then highlight it with Christmas Red.

10 Completed ribbons surrounding the oval.

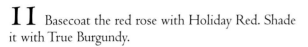

11 Basecoat the red rose with Holiday Red. Shade it with True Burgundy.

12 Highlight the red rose with Christmas Red, then Poppy Red. Concentrate the highlight on the right side of the flower.

13 Basecoat the yellow rose with Medium Yellow. Shade it with Dark Yellow. Basecoat all the leaves and stems with Hauser Green Light.

14 Highlight the yellow rose with Sunny Yellow, then Lemonade. Concentrate the highlight on the right side of the blossom.

15 Use Yellow Ochre to add more shading to the yellow rose.

16 Shade the leaves and stems with Hauser Green Medium. Basecoat the heart with Christmas Red, then shade it with Holiday Red. Basecoat the border surrounding the oval with Medium Yellow.

17 Deepen the shading on the leaves and stems with Shamrock. Highlight with Lime Light.

18 Basecoat the bluebells with French Blue. Shade with Sterling Blue.

19 Deepen the shading with a touch of True Burgundy. Highlight with Ballet Pink.

20 Basecoat the cupid's flesh with Peach Perfection. Shade it with Dark Peach Perfection. Basecoat the hair with Nutmeg.

21 Basecoat the wings with Ballet Pink, then highlight with Wicker White. Shade with French Blue. Highlight the cupid's flesh with Skintone, then with Ballet Pink. Outline features with Nutmeg.

Using the ⅛-inch (3mm) rake, highlight the hair with Yellow Ochre, then with Medium Yellow.

22 Paint the whites of the eyes with Ballet Pink. Paint the irises with Sterling Blue and the lips with Christmas Red.

23 Basecoat the background of the design within the oval with Basil Green.

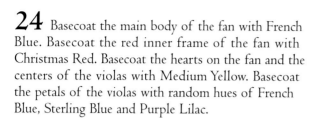

24 Basecoat the main body of the fan with French Blue. Basecoat the red inner frame of the fan with Christmas Red. Basecoat the hearts on the fan and the centers of the violas with Medium Yellow. Basecoat the petals of the violas with random hues of French Blue, Sterling Blue and Purple Lilac.

25 Shade the yellow heart with Dark Yellow, then with Yellow Ochre. Shade the red inner frame motif on the fan with Holiday Red. Shade the violas with random hues of Sterling Blue, Holiday Red, Medium Yellow and Purple Lilac.

Using the JS-2 liner, outline the fan with Sterling Blue and then with a thinner line of Holiday Red. Dot the blue body of the fan with Baby Blue.

26 Add Nutmeg shading to the left side of the yellow rose.

Basecoat cupid's diaper with French Blue. Shade it with Sterling Blue, then highlight it with Baby Blue.

Add a wash of Medium Yellow to cupid's wings. Highlight with Lemonade and then with Wicker White.

Paint some stray Nutmeg hairs on cupid's head to avoid that "helmet head" look.

Michelle's Design Secrets

TO MAKE A DESIGN POP OFF THE SURFACE, CHOOSE A BACKGROUND COLOR THAT IS EITHER SEVERAL DEGREES LIGHTER OR SEVERAL DEGREES DARKER THAN THE LIGHTEST OR DARKEST VALUE IN THE DESIGN. WHEN THE DESIGN HAS A WIDE RANGE OF VALUES, AS THIS ONE DOES, CHOOSE A BACKGROUND COLOR THAT IS EITHER HIGHER OR LOWER IN INTENSITY. THE BASIL GREEN BACKGROUND OF THIS PIECE WORKS AS A NEUTRAL THAT ENHANCES BUT DOES NOT COMPETE WITH THE MAIN DESIGN.

27 Finished cupid.

28 Dot the blue body of the fan with Sterling Blue and Purple Lilac.

29 Dot the red inner frame motif on the fan with True Burgundy.

30 Varnish with several coats of FolkArt Artists' Varnish Matte, allowing each coat to dry before adding the next.

Resources

Artograph, Inc.
2838 Vicksburg Lane N.
Plymouth, MN 55447
(888) 975-9555
www.artograph.com

Artograph is the premier manufacturer of light boxes and opaque projectors. These items are worthwhile investments. They seem to last forever and will cut your pattern transfer time in half. With their large product line, they truly have a product for every budget. Some fabulous bargains can be found on the "garage sale" page of their Web site. Artograph products can be found at art and craft retailers nationwide.

F & W Publications, Inc.
4700 E. Galbraith Rd.
Cincinnati, OH 45236
(800) 289-0963
www.artistsnetwork.com

F & W publishes my favorite art magazines including *The Artist's Magazine* and *Decorative Artist's Workbook*. They also run two wonderful book clubs for artists: North Light Book Club for fine art and Decorative Artist's Book Club for decorative painting. Purchase your art instruction books through the clubs to save 20% or more off the retail price. They also offer free shipping, an informative newsletter and great sign-up deals. Click *book clubs* at their Web site.

Also, be sure to spend time at their Web site, which is packed with hints, tips, art instruction articles and even an art clinic. While you are visiting the site, sign up for the free email newsletters filled with great tips.

Loew-Cornell, Inc.
563 Chestnut Ave.
Teaneck, NJ 07666
www.loew-cornell.com

Loew-Cornell manufactures a huge range of quality paint brushes. Whether you paint in watercolors, oils, acrylics, etc., Loew-Cornell has a brush for you. Their unique line of specialty brushes makes painting special effects easy even for the beginning painter. Their flats, rounds and angles are work horses and should be part of every painter's core supplies. Look for Loew-Cornell products at art and craft retailers nationwide. Be sure to visit their Web site which has helpful articles as well as a free teacher locator service that can help you find a teacher in your area.

Masterson Art Products. Inc.
P.O. Box 10775
Glendale, AZ 85318
(800) 965-2675
www.mastersonart.com

Every acrylic painter should be using a Masterson Sta-Wet palette. Acrylic paint dries very quickly on a regular palette, causing wasted paint, wasted money and, most importantly, poor quality paintings. Unless the acrylic paint remains at the proper moist consistency, it drags and clumps on the painting surface, creating a mess instead of a beautiful painting. The Masterson Sta-Wet palette keeps paints moist and at the proper consistency for weeks. Several of the palettes can also be used for watercolors and oils. The Handy Sta-Wet palette is particularly good for travel.

Plaid Enterprises, Inc.
P.O. Box 2835
Norcross, GA 30091-2835
www.plaidonline.com
(800) 842-4197

Plaid is the manufacturer of the wonderfully rich and creamy FolkArt acrylic paint, easy-to-use varnishes, and a plethora of wonderful supplies. Their home décor craft products are the best available. Visit the Web site to learn about the vast range of products offered by this company. Their products are conveniently available at art and craft stores nationwide.

Porcelain by Marilyn and Lavonne
3687 W. U.S. 40
Greenfield, IN 46140
(317) 462-5063

Marilyn and Lavonne manufacture beautiful and unique porcelain surfaces of every kind, including tea sets, ornaments, jewelry boxes and more. The bisque surfaces can be painted with acrylics or oils and then varnished for a glass-like finish. No firing is needed. Functional items, such as tea sets, are waterproof on the inside so that they not only look pretty on display but also can be used. Their kitchen canister sets and children's tea services are especially lovely.

Viking Woodcrafts, Inc.
1317 8th Street SE
Waseca, MN 56093
(800) 328-0116
www.vikingwoodcrafts.com

Don't miss checking out this top-quality supplier of hundreds of decorative painting surfaces, books and supplies. Viking Woodcrafts not only sells a huge assortment of wood surfaces, but also sells other surfaces including metal, canvas, glass, papier-mâché and more. Their pieces are beautiful and their Internet and mail order service is top notch.

Walnut Hollow Farm, Inc.
1409 State Road 23
Dodgeville, WI 53533
(800) 500-5101
www.walnuthollow.com

Walnut Hollow specializes in classic and innovative wood surfaces for painters. Quality and prices are both excellent. Their line of ready-to-paint clock surfaces and clock parts is unmatched by any other manufacturer. Walnut Hollow products can be found at art and craft retailers nationwide. Check out their Web site for great bargains on closeouts.

Winsor & Newton
P.O. Box 1396
Piscataway, NJ 08855
www.winsornewton.com

Winsor & Newton has been manufacturing art supplies since 1832. To stay in business this long, they'd have to make products of exceptional quality—and they do. You can't go wrong buying any Winsor & Newton product. Their watercolor paper is simply the best.

Make sure to visit the Winsor & Newton Web site and plan to spend a good bit of time there. It is overflowing with art-making tips and hints, painting lessons, product information and even a "Creative Encyclopedia." One of the best art sites on the net.

Index

A

Accents, adding, 109
Acetate, prepared, 13, 115
Aluminum foil texture, 67
Analogous color scheme, 56
Anemone, 79
Angle brush, for background, 72
Animals, references, 27

B

Backgrounds
  color intensity of, 122
  plastic wrap technique, 100, 116
  techniques for, 66–73
  texture and value, 65
Balance, 18
Blending gel, 72
Bluebells, 120
Border violation, 95, 111
Box, 83–93
Brush blending, 77
Brushes, 14
  for backgrounds, 70–72
Brush textures, 70–72
Butterfly, 108

C

Canvas, advantages and
  disadvantages, 33
Center of interest, 39
Clip art, 48
Color
  and color schemes, properties of,
    56–57
  creating mood with, 61
  as design element, 19
  floated, 74
Colored pencils, 13
Color references, 29
Color scheme
  choosing final plan, 64
  properties of, 56–57
  triadic, 111
Color studies, 62–63, 99, 114–115
  reducing pattern for, 114
Color wheel, 55
Complementary color scheme, 57, 111

Composition, 26
  classic choices, 42–43
  do's and don'ts, 37–41
  making final decision, 47
  steps to designing, 45
Compound tracing, 50
Computer-aided tracing, 51
Copyright, and reference material, 31
Copyright-free art. See Clip art
C shape, 42
Cupid, 121

D

Decorative Painter's C.E.O.™, 20–23
  combining references from, 114
Deerfoot stippler, 70, 88, 117
Design
  choosing best background, 73
  seven-step, 81
  strategies for boxlike shapes, 83
  tips, 54
  See also Composition
Design, good
  achieving, 18–19
  characteristics of, 16–17
Design, planning for, 20, 22
  box, 86–87
  secretary, 114–115
  tray, 98–99
Detail references, 28
Drawing
  from scratch, 52–53
  shortcuts, 48
Dry brushing, 78

E

Eraser, 11

F

Fabric, advantages and disadvantages, 34
Fan, 122–123
Flat brush, for background, 72
Floated color, 74
Floral references, 27
Forget-me-nots, 100–101

G

Glass, advantages and disadvantages, 33
Golden Mean, 39
Graph vellum, 12

H

Harmony, 19
Highlighting
  butterfly, 108
  Cupid, 121
  flower, 103–105, 107, 118
  letters, 91–92
  sparing use of, 111

I

Ideas, 20–21
Inspiration, 20–21

L

Lead holder and leads, 11
Leaves, deciding color for, 99
Lettering, 90–92
  matching with design, 41
Light, for reference photos, 24–25
Light box, 15
Lily, 77
Line, 18
L shape, 44

M

Marbleizing, 72
Masterson Sta-Wet palette, 14
Metal, advantages and disadvantages, 32
Mixed media, advantages and
  disadvantages, 34
Monochromatic color scheme, 56
Mood, creating with color, 61
Motif references, 28
Motifs, pulling from main design, 44

N

Negative space, 39
Notebook, loose-leaf, 15

O

Opaque projectors, 51

P

Paint, 14
    consistency, 77
Paint chips, organizing, 60
Painting, traditional vs. decorative, 6
Painting techniques, 76–79
    deciding which to use, 74–75
    See also Background techniques,
    Highlighting, Shading
Palette knife, 15
Palettes
    in Decorative Painter's C.E.O.™,
    20, 22
    Masterson Sta-Wet, 14
Pansy, 76
Paper, 12–13
    transfer, 15
Paper towels, 15
Papier mache, advantages and
    disadvantages, 34
Pattern, reducing for studies, 114
Pencils, 11
    colored, 13
Peony, 78, 104, 107
People, references, 27
Photos
    reference vs. personal, 24–25
    tracing, 49
Plastic wrap texture, 67–69, 100, 116
Play-Doh techniques, 73
Porcelain, advantages and
    disadvantages, 33
Positive space, 39
Prepared acetate, 13, 115
Proportion, 18
Proportional wheel, 54

R

Rake, for background, 70
Reference material
    capturing many types, 26–29
    organizing, 30–31
    tips for taking photos, 24–25
    using to choose color scheme, 59
    where to find, 24
Resources, 124–125
Rhythm, 18
Roses, 103
    red, 118
    yellow, 119
Ruler, 12

S

Scenic references, 26
Scrollwork, 89
    accenting, 90
Seasonal references, 28
Secretary, upright, 110–123
Shading
    butterfly, 108
    flower, 103, 106, 118–120
    letters, 91–92
    scrollwork, 90
Sharpener, 11
Sketchbook, practice, 48
Sketches, 20, 22
Slide holder sheets, 15
Spattering, 70–71
Split complementary color scheme, 58
Sponge texture, 66
S shape, 43
Stippling, 88, 117
Studies, 20, 23
    reducing pattern for, 114
    value and color, 62–63
    See also Thumbnail sketches
Supplies, 10–15
    Decorative Painter's C.E.O.™, 23
    drawing, 52
    miscellaneous, 15
Surfaces, 7
    choosing type, 32–34
    designing on largest plane of, 44
    where to purchase, 35–36

T

Template, making, 45
Texture, 19
    background, 65–72
Texture references, 29
Thumbnail sketches, 114
    developing, 46
Tracing, 49–51
Tracing paper, 12
Transfer paper, wax-free, 15
Tray, 94–109
Triad, 58
Triangular shape, 42
Tulip, 102, 106

U

Unblended technique, 79

V

Values
    background, 65, 122
    contrasting, 111
Value studies, 62–63
    reducing pattern for, 114

Water basins, 15
Water blending, 76
Watercolor paper, 13
Water effect, 69
Wood, advantages and disadvantages, 32

North Light has the answers to all your painting questions!